the complete book of

cupcakes
&
baking

This book is published by Octopus Publishing Group Limited
based on materials licensed to it by
ACP Magazines Ltd, a division of
PBL Media Pty Limited
54 Park St, Sydney
GPO Box 4088, Sydney, NSW 2001
phone (02) 9282 8618;
fax (02) 9267 9438
acpbooks@acpmagazines.com.au; www.acpbooks.com.au

OCTOPUS BOOKS
Design: Chris Bell
Food Director: Pamela Clark

This edition published specially for WHS by
Octopus Publishing Group Limited
Endeavour House
189 Shaftesbury Avenue
London WC2H 8JY
United Kingdom
phone + 44 (0) 207 632 5400;
fax + 44 (0) 207 632 5405
aww@octopusbooks.co.uk;
www.octopusbooks.co.uk
www.australian-womens-weekly.com

Printed and bound in China

International foreign language rights, Brian Cearnes, ACP Books
bcearnes@acpmagazines.com.au

A catalogue record for this book is available from the British Library.

ISBN 978-1-907428-09-8

© ACP Magazines Ltd 2010

ABN 18 053 273 546

THE AUSTRALIAN
Women's Weekly

the complete book of

cupcakes
&
baking

contents

Baking must be one of life's most rewarding efforts: the unmistakable aroma of something gently bubbling away in the oven, the crispy bits to nibble on when it's cooked and the fun of decorating and serving your creation! However agile you are (or are not) at cake decorating, just about anything can be redeemed with a dusting of icing sugar or cocoa powder or one of our wonderful icing mixtures. The most difficult decision will undoubtedly be which of our goodies to choose first. Whichever it is – enjoy!

Pamela Clark

Food Director

cupcakes & muffins

It's not so long ago when cupcakes were considered children's party fare, and if they were to grace the afternoon tea table they were dressed up as fairy or butterfly cakes, but in recent years cupcakes have grown up and become sophisticated stars of the cake kingdom. Originally a breakfast food, muffins are now a popular snack to be enjoyed with a cup of tea or coffee at any time of day. Available in both sweet and savoury versions, they can be served hot, warm or cold, with or without butter.

quick-mix cupcakes

125g butter, softened
½ teaspoon vanilla extract
¾ cup (165g) caster sugar
3 eggs
2 cups (300g) self-raising flour
¼ cup (60ml) milk

1 Preheat oven to 180°C/160°C fan-assisted. Line two 12-hole muffin pans with paper cases.
2 Combine ingredients in medium bowl; beat with electric mixer on low speed until ingredients are just combined. Increase speed to medium; beat about 3 minutes or until mixture is smooth and paler in colour.
3 Drop rounded tablespoons of mixture into each case; bake about 20 minutes. Stand cakes 5 minutes; turn, top-sides up, onto wire racks to cool.
4 Top cakes with glacé icing of your choice.

makes 24

VARIATIONS
chocolate & orange Stir in 1 teaspoon finely grated orange rind and ½ cup (95g) dark chocolate chips at the end of step 2.
passionfruit & lime Stir in 1 teaspoon finely grated lime rind and ¼ cup (60ml) passionfruit pulp at the end of step 2.
banana & white choc chip Stir in ½ cup (115g) over-ripe mashed banana and ½ cup (95g) white chocolate chips at the end of step 2.
mocha Blend 1 tablespoon sifted cocoa powder with 1 tablespoon strong black coffee; stir in at the end of step 2.

glacé icing

2 cups (320g) icing sugar
20g butter, melted
2 tablespoons hot water, approximately

1 Place sifted icing sugar in small bowl; stir in butter and enough of the hot water to make a firm paste; stir over small saucepan of simmering water until spreadable.

VARIATIONS
chocolate Stir in 1 teaspoon sifted cocoa powder.
coffee Dissolve 1 teaspoon instant coffee granules in the hot water.
passionfruit Stir in 1 tablespoon passionfruit pulp.

coconut cupcakes

125g unsalted butter, softened
1 teaspoon finely grated lemon
　rind
¾ cup (165g) caster sugar
2 eggs
½ cup (40g) desiccated coconut
1¼ cups (185g) self-raising flour
½ cup (125ml) milk
2 tablespoons desiccated coconut,
　extra
pink icing
1¼ cups (200g) icing sugar, sifted
1 tablespoon boiling water,
　approximately
pink food colouring

1 Preheat oven to 180°C/160°C fan-assisted. Line 12-hole (80ml) muffin pan with paper cases.
2 Beat butter, rind and sugar in small bowl with electric mixer until light and fluffy. Beat in eggs, one at a time. Transfer mixture to large bowl; stir in desiccated coconut, sifted flour, and milk in two batches.
3 Divide mixture into paper cases; bake about 30 minutes. Stand cupcakes in pan 5 minutes before turning, top-side up, onto wire rack to cool.
4 Make pink icing. Spread icing over cold cupcakes; sprinkle with extra coconut.
pink icing Sift icing sugar into small bowl; stir in enough water to make icing spreadable. Tint pink with colouring.

makes 12

440g can crushed pineapple in syrup
1 cup (150g) plain flour
½ cup (75g) self-raising flour
½ teaspoon bicarbonate of soda
½ teaspoon ground cinnamon
½ teaspoon ground ginger
1 cup (220g) firmly packed brown sugar
½ cup (40g) desiccated coconut
1 cup (230g) mashed over-ripe banana
2 eggs, beaten lightly
¾ cup (180ml) vegetable oil

coconut crust

3 cups (225g) shredded coconut
½ cup (110g) firmly packed brown sugar
3 eggs, beaten lightly

1 Preheat oven to 180°C/160°C fan-assisted. Line three six-hole (80ml) muffin pans with paper cases.
2 Drain pineapple over medium bowl, pressing with spoon to extract as much syrup as possible. Reserve ¼ cup of the syrup.
3 Sift flours, soda, spices and sugar into large bowl. Stir in drained pineapple, reserved syrup, coconut, banana, egg and oil. Divide mixture among paper cases. Bake cakes 10 minutes.

4 Meanwhile, make coconut crust by combining ingredients in medium bowl. Spoon crust over cakes; return to oven, bake about 15 minutes.
5 Stand cakes 5 minutes before turning, top-side up, onto wire rack to cool. Serve lightly dusted with sifted icing sugar.

makes 18
tip You will need two large (460g) over-ripe bananas to get the required amount of mashed banana.

hummingbird cupcakes with coconut crust

chocolate coconut cupcakes

⅔ cup (150g) firmly packed brown
  sugar
¼ cup (25g) cocoa powder
½ cup (75g) self-raising flour
½ cup (75g) plain flour
⅓ cup (25g) desiccated coconut
125g butter, melted
1 egg
⅓ cup (80ml) milk
chocolate butter cream
70g butter, softened
1 tablespoon milk
¾ cup (120g) icing sugar
2 tablespoons cocoa powder,
  sifted

1 Preheat oven to 160°C/140°C fan-assisted. Grease 6-hole large (180ml) muffin pan.
2 Sift sugar, cocoa and flours in medium bowl; stir in coconut, butter and combined egg and milk. Divide mixture among muffin pan holes; bake about 35 minutes. Stand 5 minutes; turn onto wire rack to cool.
3 Make chocolate butter cream; spread over cold cakes.
chocolate butter cream Beat ingredients in small bowl with electric mixer until light and fluffy.

makes 6

dark mud cake
85g butter, chopped coarsely
75g dark eating chocolate,
    chopped coarsely
⅔ cup (150g) caster sugar
½ cup (125ml) milk
½ cup (75g) plain flour
¼ cup (35g) self-raising flour
1 tablespoon cocoa powder
1 egg
white mud cake
85g butter, chopped coarsely
75g white eating chocolate,
    chopped coarsely
½ cup (110g) caster sugar
⅓ cup (80ml) milk
⅔ cup (100g) plain flour
¼ cup (35g) self-raising flour
1 egg
dark chocolate ganache
⅓ cup (80ml) double cream
200g dark eating chocolate,
    chopped coarsely
white chocolate ganache
2 tablespoons double cream
100g white eating chocolate,
    chopped coarsely

1 Preheat oven to 160°C/140°C fan-assisted. Grease two six-hole (180ml) large muffin pans.
2 Make dark mud cake by combining butter, chocolate, sugar and milk in medium saucepan; stir over low heat until smooth. Transfer to medium bowl; cool 10 minutes. Whisk in sifted flours and cocoa, then egg.
3 Make white mud cake by combining butter, chocolate, sugar and milk in medium saucepan; stir over low heat until smooth. Transfer to medium bowl; cool 10 minutes. Whisk in sifted flours, then egg.
4 Drop alternate spoonfuls of mixtures into pan holes. Pull skewer back and forth through cake mixture several times for a marbled effect. Bake about 30 minutes.
5 Meanwhile, make dark chocolate and white chocolate ganaches.
6 Stand cakes 5 minutes before turning, top-side up, onto wire rack to cool.
7 Spread cakes with dark chocolate ganache; dollop cakes with spoonfuls of white chocolate ganache. Using palette knife, swirl back and forth through ganache for marbled effect.

dark chocolate ganache Stir cream and chocolate in small saucepan over low heat until smooth. Cool 15 minutes.
white chocolate ganache Stir cream and chocolate in small saucepan over low heat until smooth. Cool 15 minutes.

makes 12

marbled chocolate mud cupcakes

berries & cream cupcakes

3 eggs
½ cup (110g) caster sugar
¼ cup (35g) cornflour
¼ cup (35g) plain flour
¼ cup (35g) self-raising flour
300ml whipping cream
pink food colouring
5 large strawberries, sliced
200g fresh blueberries
150g fresh raspberries
icing sugar, for dusting

1 Preheat oven to 180°C/160°C fan-assisted. Line 10 holes of 12-hole muffin pan with paper cases.
2 Beat eggs in small bowl with electric mixer about 5 minutes or until thick and creamy; gradually add caster sugar, one tablespoon at a time, beating until sugar dissolves between additions. Transfer to large bowl.
3 Sift the dry ingredients twice, then sift over egg mixture; fold ingredients together.
4 Drop ¼ cup of mixture into each of the paper cases. Bake cakes about 25 minutes. Turn out immediately onto wire rack, then turn cakes top-side up to cool.

5 Meanwhile, colour unwhipped chilled whipping cream pale pink. Whip the cream until it barely holds its shape.
6 Top each cake with a generous layer of the cream and a mixture of the berries. Dust the berries with a little sifted icing sugar before serving.

makes 10
tip You can use any assortment of berries and soft fruits on these cupcakes – try slices of fresh peach and raspberries, blueberries and sliced banana or fresh mango and cubes of pineapple. Remember to colour the cream to match your choice fo fruit.

raspberry & apple cupcakes

125g butter, softened
1 teaspoon vanilla extract
¾ cup (165g) caster sugar
2 eggs
1½ cups (225g) self-raising flour
½ cup (125ml) milk
150g fresh or frozen raspberries
1 large apple (200g), peeled,
    chopped finely
2 teaspoons icing sugar

1 Preheat oven to 180°C/160°C fan-assisted. Line 12-hole (80ml) muffin pan with paper cases.
2 Beat butter, extract and sugar in small bowl with electric mixer until light and fluffy. Beat in eggs, one at a time. Stir in sifted flour and milk, in two batches. Stir in raspberries and apple.
3 Divide mixture into paper cases; bake about 30 minutes. Stand cakes in pan 5 minutes before turning, top-side up, onto wire rack to cool. Dust with sifted icing sugar.

makes 12
tip If using frozen raspberries, use them straight from the freezer as thawed berries will bleed colour through the cake mix.

candy cupcakes

80g butter, softened
¼ teaspoon vanilla extract
⅓ cup (75g) caster sugar
2 eggs
1 cup (150g) self-raising flour
2 tablespoons milk
80g mini boiled sweets

1 Preheat oven to 180°C/160°C fan-assisted. Line 12-hole (40ml) deep flat-based patty pan with paper cases.
2 Combine butter, extract, sugar, eggs, sifted flour and milk in small bowl; beat with electric mixer on low speed until ingredients are combined. Increase speed to medium; beat about 2 minutes or until mixture is smooth and paler in colour.

3 Divide mixture between paper cases; bake 15 minutes. Remove cakes from oven; sprinkle sweets over cakes. Bake a further 5 minutes or until sweets melt. Stand cakes in pan 5 minutes before turning, top-side up, onto wire rack to cool.

makes 12

coffee caramel cupcakes

125g butter, softened
⅔ cup (150g) firmly packed brown sugar
2 tablespoons instant coffee powder
1 tablespoon boiling water
2 eggs
2 cups (300g) self-raising flour
½ cup (125ml) milk
18 (130g) caramel sweets, halved

1 Preheat oven to 180°C/160°C fan-assisted. Grease 12-hole (80ml) muffin pan.

2 Beat butter and sugar in small bowl with electric mixer until light and fluffy. Add combined coffee and the water, then beat in eggs, one at a time, beating until just combined between additions. Transfer mixture to large bowl.
3 Stir in sifted flour and milk. Spoon mixture into prepared pan. Press 3 caramel halves into the centre of each cake; cover with batter.
4 Bake about 20 minutes. Cool in pan 5 minutes; turn cakes onto wire racks to cool.

makes 12

banana cupcakes
with maple cream frosting

60g butter, softened
60g soft cream cheese
¾ cup (165g) firmly packed brown
    sugar
2 eggs
½ cup (125ml) milk
2 tablespoons maple syrup
1½ cups (225g) self-raising flour
½ teaspoon bicarbonate of soda
2 medium bananas (400g), halved
    lengthways, sliced thinly
maple cream frosting
30g butter, softened
80g soft cream cheese
2 tablespoons maple syrup
1½ cups (240g) icing sugar

1 Preheat oven to 180°C/160°C fan-assisted. Line 12-hole (80ml) muffin pan with paper cases.
2 Beat butter, cream cheese and sugar in medium bowl with electric mixer until light and fluffy. Beat in eggs, one at a time. Stir in milk, syrup and sifted dry ingredients; fold in bananas.
3 Drop ¼ cups of mixture into each paper case; bake about 30 minutes. Stand cakes in pans 5 minutes before turning, top-side up, onto wire rack to cool.
4 Meanwhile, make maple cream frosting. Spread cakes with frosting.
maple cream frosting Beat butter, cream cheese and syrup in small bowl with electric mixer until light and fluffy; beat in sifted icing sugar, in two batches, until combined.

makes 12

4 egg whites
125g butter, melted
⅔ cup (80g) ground almonds
¾ cup (120g) icing sugar
¼ cup (35g) plain flour
100g dark eating chocolate,
    chopped finely
¼ cup (60ml) double cream
100g dark eating chocolate,
    chopped, extra

1 Preheat oven to 200°C/180°C fan-assisted. Grease two 12-hole mini (40ml) muffin pans.
2 Place egg whites in a medium bowl; beat with a fork. Stir in butter, ground almonds, sifted icing sugar and flour and chopped chocolate. Spoon mixture into pan holes.
3 Bake cakes about 15 minutes. Stand in pans 5 minutes before turning, top-side up, onto wire rack to cool.
4 Meanwhile, combine cream and extra chocolate in small heatproof bowl over small saucepan of simmering water; stir until smooth. Stand until thick. Spoon chocolate mixture over cupcakes.

makes 24

mini choc chip & almond cupcakes

banana blueberry cupcakes

125g butter
½ cup (125ml) milk
2 eggs
1 cup (220g) caster sugar
½ cup (115g) mashed over-ripe
    banana
1½ cups (225g) self-raising flour
½ cup (75g) frozen blueberries

1 Preheat oven to 180°C/160°C
fan-assisted. Grease 12-hole (80ml)
muffin pan.
2 Place butter and milk in small
saucepan; stir over low heat until
butter melts.
3 Beat eggs in small bowl with
electric mixer until thick and creamy.
Gradually add sugar, beating until
dissolved between additions;
stir in banana. Fold in sifted flour
and cooled butter mixture, in two
batches. Divide mixture among
muffin pan holes.

4 Bake cakes 10 minutes. Remove
pan from oven; press frozen
blueberries into tops of cakes.
Return cakes to oven, bake further
15 minutes. Turn cakes onto wire
racks to cool.

makes 12
tip You will need about one large
(230g) over-ripe banana for this
recipe.

gluten-free berry cupcakes

125g butter, softened
2 teaspoons finely grated lemon
    rind
¾ cup (165g) caster sugar
4 eggs
2 cups (240g) ground almonds
½ cup (40g) desiccated coconut
½ cup (100g) rice flour
1 teaspoon bicarbonate of soda
1 cup (150g) frozen mixed berries
1 tablespoon desiccated coconut,
    extra

1 Preheat oven to 180°C/160°C
fan-assisted. Grease 12-hole (80ml)
muffin pan.
2 Beat butter, rind and sugar in
small bowl with electric mixer until
light and fluffy. Add eggs, one at a
time, beating until just combined
between additions; transfer to
large bowl. Stir in ground almonds,
coconut, sifted flour and soda, then
the berries.
3 Divide mixture among muffin
pan holes; bake about 25 minutes.
Stand cupcakes 5 minutes; turn,
top-sides up, onto wire rack to cool.
Sprinkle with extra coconut.

makes 12

carrot & orange cupcakes

⅔ cup (160ml) vegetable oil
¾ cup (165g) firmly packed brown
  sugar
2 eggs
1 teaspoon finely grated orange
  rind
1½ cups (210g) firmly packed
  coarsely grated carrot
1¾ cups (260g) self-raising flour
¼ teaspoon bicarbonate of soda
1 teaspoon mixed spice
orange glacé icing
2 cups (320g) icing sugar
20g butter, melted
2 tablespoons orange juice,
  approximately

1 Preheat oven to 180°C/160°C fan-assisted. Line 12-hole (80ml) muffin pan with paper cases.
2 Beat oil, sugar, eggs and rind in small bowl with electric mixer until thick and creamy. Transfer mixture to large bowl; stir in carrot, then sifted dry ingredients.
3 Divide mixture into paper cases; bake about 30 minutes. Stand cakes in pan 5 minutes before turning, top-side up, onto wire rack to cool.
4 Meanwhile, make orange glacé icing. Spread cakes with icing.
orange glacé icing Sift icing sugar into small heatproof bowl; stir in butter and enough juice to make a firm paste. Stir over small saucepan of simmering water until spreadable.

makes 12
tip You need about two medium carrots (240g) to get the amount of grated carrot required for this recipe.

chocolate raspberry dessert muffins

1¾ cups (260g) self-raising flour
¼ cup (25g) cocoa powder
¾ cup (165g) caster sugar
50g butter, melted
⅔ cup (160ml) milk
½ cup (120g) soured cream
2 eggs
½ cup (70g) coarsely chopped
  roasted hazelnuts
150g dark eating chocolate,
  chopped coarsely
1 cup (150g) frozen raspberries

1 Preheat oven to 200°C/180°C fan-assisted. Line 12-hole (80ml) muffin pan with paper cases.
2 Sift flour, cocoa and sugar into large bowl. Stir in the combined butter, milk, soured cream and eggs. Do not over-mix; mixture should be lumpy. Stir in remaining ingredients.
3 Divide mixture among paper cases. Bake about 20 minutes. Stand muffins 5 minutes before turning, top-side up, onto wire rack to cool.

makes 12

tips These muffins are best served warm. We used freeform paper cases made by pushing a 12cm square of paper (we used paper about the same thickness as printer paper) into ungreased pan holes, followed by a 12cm square of baking parchment.

triple choc muffins

1¾ cups (260g) self-raising flour
½ cup (50g) cocoa powder
¾ cup (165g) firmly packed brown
  sugar
½ cup (95g) dark chocolate chips
½ cup (95g) white chocolate chips
2 eggs
1 cup (250ml) buttermilk
⅔ cup (160ml) vegetable oil
12 white chocolate buttons

1 Preheat oven to 200°C/180°C fan-assisted. Line 12-hole (80ml) muffin pan with paper cases.
2 Sift flour and cocoa into large bowl; stir in sugar and chocolate chips. Stir in combined eggs, buttermilk and oil. Do not over-mix; mixture should be lumpy.
3 Divide mixture into paper cases. Bake muffins 20 minutes; remove from oven. Top each muffin with a chocolate button; bake a further 2 minutes.
4 Stand muffins in pan 5 minutes before turning, top-side up, onto wire rack to cool.

makes 12

choc-brownie muffins

2 cups (300g) self-raising flour
⅓ cup (35g) cocoa powder
⅓ cup (75g) caster sugar
60g butter, melted
½ cup (95g) chocolate chips
½ cup (75g) pistachios, chopped
   coarsely
½ cup (165g) chocolate hazelnut
   spread
1 egg, beaten lightly
¾ cup (180ml) milk
½ cup (120g) soured cream

1 Preheat oven to 200°C/180°C fan-assisted. Grease 12-hole (80ml) muffin pan.
2 Sift dry ingredients into large bowl; stir in remaining ingredients.
3 Divide mixture among holes of prepared pan.
4 Bake about 20 minutes. Stand muffins in pan for a few minutes before turning onto wire rack. Dust with sifted extra cocoa, if desired.

makes 12

choc-hazelnut muffins

2½ cups (375g) self-raising flour
½ teaspoon bicarbonate of soda
¼ cup (25g) cocoa powder
½ cup (100g) firmly packed brown
   sugar
125g butter, melted
2 eggs, lightly beaten
1 cup (250ml) buttermilk
1 cup (250ml) chocolate hazelnut
   spread

1 Preheat oven to 200°C/180°C fan-assisted. Grease 12-hole (80ml) muffin pan.
2 Sift dry ingredients into large bowl, stir in butter, eggs and buttermilk.
3 Divide one-third of the mixture among holes of prepared pan, top each with 1 level tablespoon of Nutella. Top with remaining mixture. Bake muffins about 20 minutes. Stand muffins 5 minutes; turn, top-side up, onto wire rack to cool.

makes 12

2 cups (300g) self-raising flour
⅓ cup (50g) plain flour
1 teaspoon ground cinnamon
½ teaspoon bicarbonate of soda
½ cup (110g) firmly packed brown
 sugar
1 cup (230g) mashed over-ripe
 banana
2 eggs
¾ cup (180ml) buttermilk
⅓ cup (80ml) vegetable oil
½ teaspoon ground cinnamon,
 extra
cream cheese frosting
125g cream cheese, softened
¼ cup (40g) icing sugar

1 Preheat oven to 200°C/180°C fan-assisted. Grease 12-hole (80ml) muffin pan.
2 Sift flours, cinnamon, soda and sugar into large bowl; stir in banana then combined eggs, buttermilk and oil.
3 Divide mixture among pan holes; bake muffins about 20 minutes. Stand muffins in pan 5 minutes; turn onto wire rack to cool.
4 Make cream cheese frosting.
5 Spread cold muffins with frosting; sprinkle with extra cinnamon.
cream cheese frosting Beat ingredients in small bowl with electric mixer until smooth.

makes 12
tip You need about 2 large over-ripe bananas (460g) for this recipe.

banana & cinnamon muffins

berry muffins

2½ cups (375g) self-raising flour
90g cold butter, chopped
1 cup (220g) caster sugar
1¼ cups (310ml) buttermilk
1 egg, beaten lightly
200g fresh or frozen mixed berries

1 Preheat oven to 180°C/160°C fan-assisted. Grease 12-hole (80ml) muffin pan.
2 Sift flour into large bowl; rub in butter. Stir in sugar, buttermilk and egg. Do not over-mix; mixture should be lumpy. Add berries; stir through gently.
3 Spoon mixture into pan holes; bake about 20 minutes. Stand muffins 5 minutes; turn, top-side up, onto wire rack to cool.

makes 12

VARIATIONS
lemon poppy seed Omit berries. Add 2 teaspoons lemon rind and 2 tablespoons poppy seeds with the sugar.
date & orange Omit berries. Substitute self-raising flour with 1 cup wholemeal self-raising flour and 1½ cups white self-raising flour. Add 1½ cups pitted, chopped dried dates and 2 teaspoons finely grated orange rind with the sugar.
choc chip & walnut Omit mixed berries. Add ¾ cup dark chocolate chips and 1 cup coarsely chopped walnuts with the sugar.

blueberry muffins

2 cups (300g) self-raising flour
¾ cup (150g) firmly packed brown sugar
1 cup (150g) fresh or frozen blueberries
1 egg, lightly beaten
¾ cup (180ml) buttermilk
½ cup (125ml) vegetable oil

1 Preheat oven to 180°C/160°C fan-assisted. Grease 6-hole (180ml) muffin pan.
2 Sift dry ingredients into large bowl, stir in remaining ingredients.
3 Spoon mixture into prepared pan. Bake muffins about 20 minutes. Stand muffins 5 minutes; turn, top-side up, onto wire rack to cool.

makes 6

ginger & pear muffins

2 cups (300g) self-raising flour
1 teaspoon ground ginger
¾ cup (165g) caster sugar
80g butter, melted
1 cup (280g) plain yogurt
2 eggs
2 medium pears (460g), peeled,
    chopped finely
muesli topping
50g butter
2 tablespoons honey
2 cups (220g) unsweetened muesli

1 Preheat oven to 200°C/180°C fan-assisted. Line 12-hole (80ml) muffin pan with paper cases.
2 Make muesli topping.
3 Sift flour and ginger into large bowl; stir in sugar and the combined butter, yogurt and eggs. Do not over-mix; mixture should be lumpy. Gently stir in pears.
4 Spoon mixture into pan holes; spoon muesli topping onto muffin mixture. Bake about 20 minutes. Stand muffins 5 minutes before turning, top-side up, onto wire rack to cool.
muesli topping Stir butter and honey in small saucepan over low heat until combined. Remove from heat; stir in muesli.

makes 12
tips Buy a muesli that contains dried fruit to add colour and flavour to the muffins. We used freeform paper cases made by pushing a 12cm square of paper (we used paper about the same thickness as printer paper) into ungreased pan holes, followed by a 12cm square of baking parchment.

banana, cranberry & macadamia muffins

2¼ cups (335g) self-raising flour
¾ cup (165g) caster sugar
½ cup (65g) dried cranberries
½ cup (70g) coarsely chopped
   roasted unsalted macadamias
⅔ cup (135g) mashed banana
2 eggs, beaten lightly
1 cup (250ml) milk
½ cup (125ml) vegetable oil

1 Preheat oven to 200°C/180°C fan-assisted. Line three 6-hole (80ml) muffin pans with paper cases.
2 Sift flour and sugar into large bowl; stir in berries and nuts. Stir in the combined remaining ingredients; do not over-mix, mixture should be lumpy.
3 Divide mixture among pan holes. Bake about 20 minutes. Stand muffins 5 minutes before turning, top-side up, onto wire rack to cool. Serve lightly dusted with sifted icing sugar.

makes 18

tips You need two medium (400g) over-ripe bananas to get the required amount of mashed banana. We used freeform paper cases made by pushing a 12cm square of paper (we used paper about the same thickness as printer paper) into ungreased pan holes, followed by a 12cm square of baking parchment.

VARIATION

banana, raisin & pecan Omit the cranberries and replace with ½ cup coarsely chopped raisins. Omit the macadamias and replace with ½ cup coarsely chopped roasted pecans.

banana & date muffins

2 cups (300g) self-raising flour
1 teaspoon mixed spice
½ cup (100g) firmly packed brown
   sugar
1 cup (230g) mashed banana
1 cup (160g) pitted chopped dates
3 eggs, lightly beaten
⅓ cup (80ml) vegetable oil
⅓ cup (80ml) buttermilk

1 Preheat oven to 200°C/180°C fan-assisted. Grease 12-hole (80ml capacity) muffin pan.
2 Sift dry ingredients into large bowl, stir in remaining ingredients.
3 Spoon mixture into prepared pan. Bake about 20 minutes. Stand muffins 5 minutes before turning, top-side up, onto wire rack to cool.

makes 12
tip You need about 2 large over-ripe bananas (460g) for this recipe.

lime & blueberry mini muffins

3 egg whites
90g unsalted butter, melted
1 teaspoon finely grated lime rind
½ cup (60g) ground almonds
¾ cup (120g) icing sugar
¼ cup (35g) plain flour
⅓ cup (50g) frozen blueberries
1 tablespoon icing sugar, extra

1 Preheat oven to 180°C/160°C fan-assisted. Grease two 12-hole (1-tablespoon/20ml) mini muffin pans.
2 Place egg whites in medium bowl, whisk until frothy. Stir in butter, rind, ground almonds and sifted icing sugar and flour.
3 Drop heaped teaspoons of mixture into each muffin pan hole; top each with a blueberry.
4 Bake about 10 minutes. Stand muffins in pans 5 minutes; turn onto wire rack to cool.
5 Dust with sifted extra icing sugar.

makes 24

40g butter

3 large apples (600g), peeled, cut into 1cm pieces

⅓ cup (75g) firmly packed brown sugar

2 cups (300g) self-raising flour

1 teaspoon mixed spice

⅔ cup (150g) caster sugar

80g butter, melted, extra

¾ cup (180ml) buttermilk

1 egg

streusel topping

⅓ cup (50g) self-raising flour

⅓ cup (50g) plain flour

⅓ cup (75g) firmly packed brown sugar

½ teaspoon ground cinnamon

80g cold butter, chopped coarsely

1 Make streusel topping.

2 Meanwhile, melt butter in large frying pan; cook apple, stirring, about 5 minutes or until browned lightly. Add brown sugar; cook, stirring, about 5 minutes or until mixture thickens. Cool.

3 Preheat oven to 200°C/180°C fan-assisted. Line 12-hole (80ml) muffin pan with paper cases.

4 Sift flour, spice and sugar into large bowl. Stir in the combined extra butter, buttermilk and egg. Do not over-mix; mixture should be lumpy. Stir in half the apple mixture.

5 Divide mixture among pan holes; top with remaining apple mixture.

6 Coarsely grate streusel topping over muffin mixture. Bake about 20 minutes. Stand muffins 5 minutes before turning, top-side up, onto wire rack to cool.

streusel topping Process flours, sugar and cinnamon until combined. Add butter; process until combined. Roll dough into ball, wrap in cling film; freeze about 15 minutes or until firm.

makes 12

tips We used freeform paper cases made by pushing a 12cm square of paper (we used paper about the same thickness as printer paper) into ungreased pan holes, followed by a 12cm square of baking parchment.

apple streusel muffins

date muffins with orange syrup

1¼ cups (185g) white self-raising
   flour
1 cup (160g) wholemeal self-raising
   flour
1 cup (220g) caster sugar
100g butter, melted
1 cup (280g) plain yogurt
2 eggs
1 teaspoon finely grated orange
   rind
1½ cups (210g) coarsely chopped
   pitted dried dates
orange syrup
½ cup (110g) caster sugar
¼ cup (60ml) water
2 teaspoons finely grated orange
   rind
¼ cup (60ml) orange juice

1 Preheat oven to 200°C/180°C
fan-assisted. Grease 12-hole (80ml)
muffin pan with butter.
2 Sift flours and sugar into large
bowl. Stir in combined butter,
yogurt, eggs and rind. Do not over-
mix; mixture should be lumpy. Stir
in dates. Divide mixture among pan
holes. Bake about 20 minutes.
3 Meanwhile, make orange syrup.
4 Stand muffins 2 minutes before
turning, top-side up, onto wire rack.
Stand rack over tray. Pierce muffins
all over with skewer; pour hot
orange syrup over hot muffins.
orange syrup Stir ingredients in
small saucepan over heat until sugar
dissolves. Bring to the boil; reduce
heat. Simmer, uncovered, 2 minutes.

makes 12

VARIATION
fig muffins with orange syrup
Omit the dates and replace them
with 1 cup coarsely chopped
dried figs.

butterscotch pecan muffins

¾ cup (240g) dulce de leche
2 cups (300g) self-raising flour
¾ cup (165g) firmly packed brown
   sugar
¾ cup (90g) coarsely chopped
   roasted pecans
80g butter, melted
1 cup (250ml) buttermilk
1 egg

1 Preheat oven to 200°C/180°C fan-assisted. Line 12-hole (80ml) muffin pan with paper cases.
2 Stir dulce de leche in small saucepan over low heat until smooth. Cool 5 minutes.
3 Meanwhile sift flour and sugar into large bowl. Stir in nuts and the combined butter, buttermilk and egg. Do not over-mix; mixture should be lumpy.
4 Divide half the mixture among paper cases. Spoon half the caramel over muffin mixture; top with remaining mixture then caramel. Using a skewer, gently swirl caramel into muffin mixture. Bake about 20 minutes. Stand muffins 5 minutes before turning, top-side up, onto wire rack to cool.

makes 12

rhubarb & custard muffins

2 cups (300g) self-raising flour
½ cup (75g) plain flour
¾ cup (165g) caster sugar
100g butter, melted
1 cup (250ml) milk
1 egg
3 cups (330g) finely chopped
   rhubarb
1 tablespoon demerara sugar
custard
2 tablespoons custard powder
¼ cup (55g) caster sugar
1 cup (250ml) milk
1 teaspoon vanilla extract

1 Make custard.
2 Preheat oven to 200°C/180°C fan-assisted. Line 12-hole (80ml) muffin pan with paper cases.
3 Sift flours and caster sugar into large bowl. Stir in the combined butter, milk and egg. Do not over-mix; mixture should be lumpy. Stir in half the rhubarb.
4 Divide half the mixture among paper cases; top with custard. Divide remaining mixture over custard. Sprinkle with remaining rhubarb and demerara sugar.

5 Bake about 25 minutes. Stand muffins 5 minutes before turning, top-side up, onto wire rack to cool. Lightly dust with sifted icing sugar.
custard Combine custard powder and sugar in small saucepan; gradually stir in milk. Stir over medium heat until custard boils and thickens. Stir in extract; cool.

makes 12
tips You need five large stems of rhubarb to get the required amount of chopped rhubarb.

rhubarb crumble muffins

2½ cups (375g) self-raising flour
130g brown sugar
100g butter, melted
1 cup (250ml) milk
1 egg, lightly beaten
rhubarb filling
1½ cups (190g) chopped rhubarb
¼ cup (55g) caster sugar
2 tablespoons water
¼ teaspoon grated lemon rind
crumble topping
¼ cup (35g) plain flour
65g brown sugar
2 tablespoons toasted muesli
1 teaspoon grated lemon rind
30g butter, melted

1 Preheat oven to 200°C/180°C fan-assisted. Grease 12-hole (80ml) muffin pan.
2 Sift dry ingredients into large bowl, stir in remaining ingredients.
3 Half-fill prepared pan with muffin mixture, spoon rhubarb filling into wells, top with remaining muffin mixture, spread carefully to cover filling. Sprinkle with crumble topping, press gently onto muffin mixture. Bake about 20 minutes. Stand muffins 5 minutes before turning, top-side up, onto wire rack to cool.

rhubarb filling Combine all ingredients in small pan, bring to boil, simmer, uncovered, 5 minutes or until mixture is thick and rhubarb soft; cool.
crumble topping Combine all ingredients in small bowl; mix well.

makes 12

maple banana muffins with coconut topping

2 cups (300g) self-raising flour
⅓ cup (50g) plain flour
½ teaspoon bicarbonate of soda
½ cup (110g) firmly packed brown sugar
¼ cup (60ml) maple-flavoured syrup
⅔ cup (135g) mashed banana
2 eggs, beaten lightly
1 cup (250ml) buttermilk
⅓ cup (80ml) vegetable oil

coconut topping
15g butter
1 tablespoon maple-flavoured syrup
⅔ cup (30g) flaked coconut

1 Preheat oven to 200°C/180°C fan-assisted. Grease 12-hole (80ml) muffin pan.
2 Make coconut topping.
3 Sift dry ingredients into large bowl. Stir in maple syrup and banana, then egg, buttermilk and oil.
4 Divide mixture among holes of prepared pan; sprinkle with coconut topping.
5 Bake about 20 minutes. Stand muffins in pan 5 minutes before turning onto wire rack to cool.

coconut topping Melt butter in small saucepan, add maple syrup and coconut; stir constantly over high heat until coconut is browned lightly. Remove from heat.

makes 12
tip You will need about two medium (400g) over-ripe bananas for this recipe.

1 cup (160g) pitted chopped dates
⅓ cup (80ml) water
¼ teaspoon bicarbonate of soda
2 cups (300g) self-raising flour
1 cup (150g) plain flour
2 teaspoons ground ginger
½ teaspoon mixed spice
1 cup (220g) firmly packed brown
   sugar
2 teaspoons grated orange rind
1 egg, beaten lightly
1¼ cups (310ml) milk
¼ cup (60ml) vegetable oil
caramel sauce
1 cup (220g) firmly packed brown
   sugar
1 cup (250ml) double cream
40g butter

1 Preheat oven to 200°C/180°C fan-assisted. Grease 12-hole (80ml) muffin pan.
2 Combine dates and water in small saucepan, bring to a boil; remove from heat, add bicarbonate of soda, stand 5 minutes.
3 Meanwhile, sift dry ingredients into large bowl, stir in date mixture and remaining ingredients.
4 Divide mixture among holes of prepared pan.
5 Bake muffins about 20 minutes. Stand muffins in pan 5 minutes before turning onto wire rack to cool. Serve warm muffins drizzled with caramel sauce.

caramel sauce Combine ingredients in medium saucepan. Stir over heat, without boiling, until sugar is dissolved, then simmer, without stirring, about 3 minutes or until thickened slightly.

makes 12

ginger date muffins with caramel sauce

marmalade almond muffins

2 cups (300g) self-raising flour
125g butter, chopped
1 cup (80g) flaked almonds
⅔ cup (150g) caster sugar
1 tablespoon finely grated orange
   rind
½ cup (170g) orange marmalade
2 eggs, beaten lightly
½ cup (125ml) milk
¼ cup (20g) flaked almonds, extra
orange syrup
¼ cup (85g) orange marmalade
2 tablespoons water

1 Preheat oven to 200°C/180°C
fan-assisted. Grease 12-hole (80ml)
muffin pan.
2 Sift flour into large bowl, rub in
butter. Stir in nuts, sugar and rind,
then marmalade, egg and milk.
3 Divide mixture among holes of
prepared pan; sprinkle with extra
nuts.

4 Bake muffins about 20 minutes.
Stand muffins in pan 5 minutes
before turning onto wire rack to
cool.
5 Meanwhile, combine orange
syrup ingredients in small bowl.
Drizzle syrup over warm muffins.

makes 12

coconut lemon syrup muffins

2 cups (300g) self-raising flour
90g butter
¾ cup (165) caster sugar
1 cup (90g) coconut
1 tablespoon grated lemon rind
1 egg, lightly beaten
1 cup (250ml) coconut cream
2 tablespoons shredded coconut
lemon syrup
½ cup (110g) caster sugar
¼ cup (60ml) water
2 teaspoons grated lemon rind
¼ cup (60ml) lemon juice

1 Preheat oven to 200°C/180°C
fan-assisted. Grease 12-hole (80ml)
muffin pan.
2 Sift flour into large bowl, rub in
butter. Stir in sugar, coconut, rind,
egg and coconut cream.
3 Spoon mixture into prepared pan,
sprinkle with shredded coconut.
Bake about 20 minutes. Pour hot
lemon syrup over hot muffins, then
turn onto wire rack to cool.

lemon syrup Combine all the
ingredients in pan, stir over
heat, without boiling, until sugar
dissolves, then simmer 2 minutes
without stirring.

makes 12

cookies, biscuits & slices

Making a slice or a few trays of cookies can be fun, is certainly easy and, goodness knows, the end result is a far better product than store-bought. Some of our recipes are rich and decadent, some simple and homely; others can double as a dessert; and most make a fabulous lunchbox discovery. Don't underestimate the impact these small morsels will create when presented – or how the scent of their baking draws an audience even before they're removed from the oven.

basic vanilla biscuits

200g butter, softened
½ teaspoon vanilla extract
1 cup (160g) icing sugar
1 egg
1¾ cups (260g) plain flour
½ teaspoon bicarbonate of soda

1 Preheat oven to 170°C/150°C fan-assisted. Grease oven trays; line with baking parchment.
2 Beat butter, extract, sifted icing sugar and egg in small bowl with electric mixer until light and fluffy. Transfer to medium bowl; stir in sifted flour and soda, in two batches.
3 Roll level tablespoons of dough into balls; place on trays 3cm apart. Bake about 15 minutes; cool biscuits on trays.

makes 30

VARIATIONS
cranberry & coconut Stir ½ cup (65g) dried cranberries and ½ cup (40g) shredded coconut into basic biscuit mixture before flour and soda are added.
pear & ginger Stir ¼ cup (35g) finely chopped dried pears, ¼ cup (55g) coarsely chopped stem ginger and ½ cup (45g) rolled oats into basic biscuit mixture before flour and soda are added.
brown sugar & pecan Substitute 1 cup (220g) firmly packed brown sugar for the icing sugar in the basic biscuit mixture. Stir ½ cup (60g) coarsely chopped pecans into basic biscuit mixture before flour and soda are added.

top: cranberry & coconut
bottom: pear & ginger
right: brown sugar & pecan

chocolate chip cookies

250g butter, softened
1 teaspoon vanilla extract
¾ cup (165g) caster sugar
¾ cup (165g) firmly packed
   brown sugar
1 egg
2¼ cups (335g) plain flour
1 teaspoon bicarbonate of soda
375g dark eating chocolate,
   chopped coarsely

1 Preheat oven to 180°C/160°C fan-assisted. Grease oven trays.
2 Beat butter, extract, sugars and egg in small bowl with electric mixer until light and fluffy. Transfer mixture to large bowl; stir in sifted flour and soda, in two batches. Stir in chocolate, cover; refrigerate 1 hour.
3 Roll level tablespoons of mixture into balls; place about 3cm apart on trays. Bake about 12 minutes; cool on trays.

makes 40
tips Dark chocolate can be replaced with milk or white chocolate. For chocolate-nut cookies, replace a third of the chocolate with roasted chopped nuts such as hazelnuts, walnuts or pecans.

triple-choc cookies

125g butter, chopped
1 teaspoon vanilla extract
1¼ cups (275g) firmly packed
   brown sugar
1 egg
1 cup (150g) plain flour
¼ cup (35g) self-raising flour
1 teaspoon bicarbonate of soda
⅓ cup (35g) cocoa powder
½ cup (85g) chopped raisins
½ cup (95g) milk chocolate chips
½ cup (75g) white chocolate chips
½ cup (75g) dark chocolate chips

1 Preheat oven to 180°C/160°C fan-assisted.
2 Beat butter, extract, sugar and egg in small bowl with electric mixer until smooth; do not overbeat. Stir in sifted dry ingredients, then raisins and all the chocolate chips.
3 Drop level tablespoons of mixture onto lightly greased oven trays, allowing 5cm between each cookie.
4 Bake cookies about 10 minutes. Stand cookies on trays 5 minutes; transfer to wire rack to cool.

makes 36

frangipane jam drops

125g butter, softened
½ teaspoon vanilla extract
½ cup (110g) caster sugar
1 cup (120g) ground almonds
1 egg
⅔ cup (100g) plain flour
2 tablespoons raspberry jam

1 Preheat oven to 180°C/160°C fan-assisted. Grease oven trays; line with baking parchment.
2 Beat butter, extract, sugar and ground almonds in small bowl with electric mixer until light and fluffy. Add egg, beating until just combined; stir in sifted flour.

3 Drop level tablespoons of mixture on trays 5cm apart. Use handle of wooden spoon to make small hole (about 1cm deep) in top of each biscuit; fill each hole with ¼ teaspoon jam. Bake about 15 minutes; cool jam drops on trays.

makes 24

jammy spice drops

30g butter
⅓ cup (115g) golden syrup
1 cup (150g) plain flour
½ teaspoon bicarbonate of soda
¼ teaspoon ground ginger
¼ teaspoon ground cardamom
¼ teaspoon ground cinnamon
¼ teaspoon ground cloves
½ teaspoon cocoa powder
1 tablespoon milk
2 tablespoons finely chopped
   mixed peel
¼ cup (80g) raspberry jam
60g dark eating chocolate, melted

1 Melt butter in small saucepan; add syrup, bring to a boil. Remove pan from heat; stand 10 minutes.
2 Stir in sifted dry ingredients, milk and peel. Cover; cool 2 hours.
3 Preheat oven to 180°C/160°C fan-assisted. Grease two oven trays.
4 Knead dough on surface dusted with a little extra flour until it loses stickiness. Roll dough between sheets of baking parchment until about 8mm thick. Cut out rounds using 4cm-fluted round cutter. Place about 3cm apart on trays.

5 Using end of handle of wooden spoon, gently press hollows into each round; fill with ½ teaspoon jam. Bake 10 minutes; cool on trays.
6 Spread flat-sides of biscuits with chocolate. Place biscuits, jam-side down, on foil-lined trays; set at room temperature.

makes 24

golden pecan twists

2 tablespoons golden syrup
⅓ cup (40g) finely chopped
　pecans
125g butter, softened
¼ teaspoon vanilla extract
⅓ cup (75g) caster sugar
1 egg yolk
1 cup (150g) plain flour

1 Preheat oven to 180°C/160°C fan-assisted. Grease oven trays; line with baking parchment.
2 Combine half of the golden syrup with nuts in small bowl.
3 Beat butter, extract, sugar, remaining golden syrup and egg yolk in small bowl with electric mixer until light and fluffy. Stir in sifted flour.

4 Shape rounded teaspoons of mixture into balls; roll each ball into 12cm log. Twist each log into a loop, overlapping one end over the other. Place twists on trays 3cm apart; top each twist with ½ teaspoon nut mixture.
5 Bake twists about 10 minutes; cool twists on trays.

makes 30

coffee almond biscuits

1 tablespoon instant coffee
　granules
3 teaspoons hot water
3 cups (360g) ground almonds
1 cup (220g) caster sugar
2 tablespoons coffee-flavoured
　liqueur
3 egg whites, beaten lightly
24 chocolate-coated coffee beans

1 Preheat oven to 180°C/160°C fan-assisted. Grease oven trays; line with baking parchment.
2 Dissolve coffee in the hot water in large bowl. Add ground almonds, sugar, liqueur and egg whites; stir until mixture forms a firm paste.
3 Roll level tablespoons of mixture into balls; place on trays 3cm apart; flatten with hand. Press coffee beans into tops of biscuits.
4 Bake about 15 minutes; cool biscuits on trays.

makes 24

crunchy muesli cookies

1 cup (90g) rolled oats
1 cup (150g) plain flour
1 cup (220g) caster sugar
2 teaspoons ground cinnamon
¼ cup (35g) dried cranberries
⅓ cup (55g) finely chopped dried
   apricots
½ cup (70g) slivered almonds
125g butter
2 tablespoons golden syrup
½ teaspoon bicarbonate of soda
1 tablespoon boiling water

1 Preheat oven to 150°C/130°C
fan-assisted. Grease oven trays;
line with baking parchment.
2 Combine oats, flour, sugar,
cinnamon, dried fruit and nuts in
large bowl.
3 Melt butter with golden syrup in
small saucepan over low heat; add
combined soda and the boiling
water. Stir warm butter mixture into
dry ingredients.

4 Roll level tablespoons of mixture
into balls, place on trays 5cm apart;
flatten with hand. Bake about
20 minutes; cool cookies on trays.

makes 36

cranberry & pistachio muesli bites

125g butter
⅓ cup (75g) firmly packed brown
   sugar
2 tablespoons honey
1½ cups (135g) rolled oats
½ cup (75g) self-raising flour
1 cup (130g) dried cranberries
1 cup (140g) toasted shelled
   pistachios, chopped coarsely

1 Preheat oven to 180°C/160°C
fan-assisted. Grease 20cm x 30cm
baking tin; line base and two long
sides with baking parchment,
extending paper 2cm above long
sides.
2 Melt butter with sugar and honey
in medium saucepan over medium
heat without boiling, stirring, until
sugar is dissolved.
3 Stir remaining ingredients into
butter mixture.
4 Press mixture firmly into tin; bake
about 20 minutes. Cool in tin before
cutting into squares.

makes 30

250g butter, softened
1 teaspoon vanilla extract
1¼ cups (200g) icing sugar
2 tablespoons finely grated lemon
  rind
½ cup (85g) polenta
2½ cups (375g) plain flour
1 tablespoon lemon juice

1 Beat butter, extract, icing sugar and 1 teaspoon of the rind in small bowl with electric mixer until combined. Stir in polenta, flour and juice, in two batches.
2 Knead dough on floured surface until smooth. Divide dough in half; shape pieces into two 20cm-long logs. Cover, refrigerate 2 hours or until firm.
3 Preheat oven to 200°C/180°C fan-assisted. Lightly grease oven trays.
4 Cut logs into 1cm slices; place, 2cm apart, on two oven trays, sprinkle remaining rind over biscuits. Bake about 15 minutes. Stand 5 minutes; turn onto wire rack to cool.

makes 40

VARIATION
orange polenta biscuits Substitute finely grated orange rind for the lemon rind in the recipe.

lemon polenta biscuits

oaty cookies

1 cup (90g) rolled oats
1 cup (150g) plain flour
1 cup (220g) firmly packed brown
  sugar
½ cup (40g) desiccated coconut
125g butter
2 tablespoons golden syrup
1 tablespoon water
½ teaspoon bicarbonate of soda

1 Preheat oven to 160°C/140°C fan-assisted. Grease oven trays; line with baking parchment.
2 Combine oats, sifted flour, sugar and coconut in large bowl. Combine butter, syrup and the water in small saucepan, stir over low heat until smooth; stir in soda. Stir into dry ingredients.
3 Roll level tablespoons of mixture into balls; place about 5cm apart on trays, flatten slightly. Bake about 20 minutes; cool on trays.

makes 25

oaty cookie bites

½ cup (45g) rolled oats
60g butter
1 tablespoon golden syrup
¼ teaspoon bicarbonate of soda
½ cup (75g) plain flour
½ cup (110g) caster sugar
⅓ cup (25g) desiccated coconut

1 Preheat oven to 150°C/130°C fan-assisted. Grease two oven trays.
2 Blend or process oats until chopped coarsely.
3 Combine butter and syrup in medium saucepan; stir over low heat until smooth. Remove pan from heat; stir in soda, then remaining ingredients.
4 Roll rounded teaspoons of the mixture into balls. Place about 5cm apart on trays; flatten slightly. Bake about 15 minutes; cool on trays.

makes 36

gingernuts

90g butter
⅓ cup (75g) firmly packed brown
  sugar
⅓ cup (115g) golden syrup
1⅓ cups (200g) plain flour
¾ teaspoon bicarbonate of soda
1 tablespoon ground ginger
1 teaspoon ground cinnamon
¼ teaspoon ground cloves

1 Preheat oven to 180°C/160°C fan-assisted. Grease oven trays.
2 Combine butter, sugar and syrup in medium saucepan; stir over low heat until smooth. Remove from heat; stir in sifted dry ingredients. Cool 10 minutes.
3 Roll rounded teaspoons of mixture into balls. Place about 3cm apart on trays; flatten slightly. Bake about 10 minutes; cool on trays.

makes 32

oat & bran biscuits

1 cup (150g) plain flour
1 cup (60g) unprocessed bran
¾ cup (60g) rolled oats
½ teaspoon bicarbonate of soda
60g butter, chopped
½ cup (110g) caster sugar
1 egg
2 tablespoons water,
  approximately

1 Process flour, bran, oats, soda and butter until crumbly; add sugar, egg and enough of the water to make a firm dough. Knead dough on lightly floured surface until smooth; cover, refrigerate 30 minutes.
2 Preheat oven to 180°C/160°C fan-assisted. Grease oven trays; line with baking parchment.
3 Divide dough in half; roll each half between sheets of baking parchment to about 5mm thickness. Cut into 7cm rounds; place on trays 2cm apart. Bake about 15 minutes. Stand biscuits on trays 5 minutes; transfer to wire rack to cool.

makes 30

orange, coconut & almond biscotti

1 cup (220g) caster sugar
2 eggs
1 teaspoon grated orange rind
1⅓ cups (200g) plain flour
⅓ cup (50g) self-raising flour
⅔ (50g) shredded coconut
1 cup (160g) blanched almonds

1 Preheat oven to 180°C/160°C fan-assisted.
2 Whisk sugar, eggs and rind together in medium bowl. Stir in sifted flours, coconut and nuts; mix to a sticky dough.
3 Knead dough on lightly floured surface until smooth. Divide dough into two portions. Using floured hands, roll each portion into a 20cm log; place logs on lightly greased oven tray.

4 Bake about 35 minutes or until browned lightly. Cool on tray 10 minutes. Reduce oven to 170°C/150°C fan-assisted.
5 Using a serrated knife, cut logs diagonally into 1cm slices. Place slices, in single layer, on ungreased oven trays.
6 Bake about 25 minutes or until dry and crisp, turning over halfway through cooking; cool on wire racks.

makes 30

anise biscotti

125g butter
¾ cup (165g) caster sugar
3 eggs
2 tablespoons brandy
1 tablespoon grated lemon rind
1½ cups (225g) plain flour
¾ cup (110g) self-raising flour
125g blanched almonds, toasted, chopped coarsely
1 tablespoon ground aniseed

1 Beat butter and sugar in large bowl with electric mixer until just combined; add eggs, one at a time, beating well after each addition. Add brandy and rind; mix well. Stir in flours, nuts and aniseed; cover, refrigerate 1 hour.
2 Preheat oven to 180°C/160°C fan-assisted.
3 Halve dough; shape each half into a 30cm log. Place on lightly greased oven tray.

4 Bake about 20 minutes or until browned lightly. Cool logs on oven tray about 10 minutes.
5 Using a serrated knife, cut logs diagonally into 1cm slices. Place slices, in single layer, on ungreased oven trays.
6 Bake about 25 minutes or until dry and crisp, turning over halfway through cooking; cool on wire racks.

makes 40

almond macaroons

2 egg whites
½ cup (110g) caster sugar
1¼ cups (150g) ground almonds
½ teaspoon almond essence
2 tablespoons plain flour
¼ cup (40g) blanched almonds

1 Preheat oven to 150°C/130°C fan-assisted. Grease oven trays.
2 Beat egg whites in small bowl with electric mixer until soft peaks form; gradually add sugar, beating until dissolved between additions. Gently fold in ground almonds, essence and sifted flour, in two batches.
3 Drop level tablespoons of mixture about 5cm apart on trays; press one nut onto each macaroon. Bake about 20 minutes or until firm and dry; cool on trays.

makes 22

VARIATIONS
coconut Replace ground almonds with ¾ cup desiccated coconut and ¾ cup shredded coconut. Replace almond essence with vanilla extract; omit blanched almonds.
strawberry coconut Replace ground almonds with 1½ cups shredded coconut. Replace almond essence with vanilla extract; omit blanched almonds. Fold ⅓ cup finely chopped dried strawberries into the basic mixture.

little apricot macaroons

¼ cup (40g) finely chopped dried apricots
1 teaspoon orange-flavoured liqueur
1 egg white
¼ cup (55g) caster sugar
1 cup (75g) desiccated coconut
1 tablespoon finely chopped white eating chocolate

1 Preheat oven to 150°C/130°C fan-assisted. Line two 12-hole (1-tablespoon/20ml) mini muffin pans with paper cases.
2 Combine apricots and liqueur in small bowl.
3 Beat egg white in another small bowl with electric mixer until soft peaks form; gradually add sugar, beating until dissolved between additions. Fold in apricot mixture, coconut and chocolate.
4 Place 1 heaped teaspoon in each paper case. Bake about 20 minutes; cool in pans.

makes 24

1¼ cups (185g) plain flour
100g butter, chopped
½ cup (110g) caster sugar
1 egg yolk
1 tablespoon milk, approximately
⅓ cup (110g) chocolate hazelnut
    spread
2 tablespoons ground hazelnuts

1 Process flour, butter and sugar until crumbly. Add egg yolk; process with enough milk until mixture forms a ball. Knead dough on lightly floured surface until smooth; cover, refrigerate 1 hour.
2 Roll dough between sheets of baking parchment to form 20cm x 30cm rectangle; remove top sheet of paper. Spread dough evenly with hazelnut spread; sprinkle with ground hazelnuts. Using paper as a guide, roll dough tightly from long side to enclose filling. Enclose roll in cling film; refrigerate 30 minutes.
3 Preheat oven to 180°C/160°C fan-assisted. Grease oven trays; line with baking parchment.
4 Remove film from dough; cut roll into 1cm slices. Place slices on trays 2cm apart. Bake about 20 minutes. Stand pinwheels on trays 5 minutes; transfer to wire rack to cool.

makes 30

hazelnut pinwheels

vanilla kisses

125g butter, softened
½ cup (110g) caster sugar
1 egg
⅓ cup (50g) plain flour
¼ cup (35g) self-raising flour
⅔ cup (100g) cornflour
¼ cup (30g) custard powder
vienna cream
60g butter, softened
½ teaspoon vanilla extract
¾ cup (120g) icing sugar
2 teaspoons milk

1 Preheat oven to 200°C/180°C fan-assisted. Grease oven trays; line with baking parchment.
2 Beat butter, sugar and egg in small bowl with electric mixer until light and fluffy. Stir in sifted dry ingredients, in two batches.
3 Spoon mixture into piping bag fitted with 1cm-fluted tube. Pipe 3cm rosettes about 3cm apart on trays. Bake about 10 minutes; cool on trays.

4 Meanwhile, make vienna cream. Sandwich biscuits with vienna cream.
vienna cream Beat butter and extract in small bowl with electric mixer until as white as possible; gradually beat in sifted icing sugar and milk, in two batches.

makes 20

chocolate melting moments

125g butter, softened
2 tablespoons icing sugar
¾ cup (110g) plain flour
2 tablespoons cornflour
1 tablespoon cocoa powder
¼ cup (85g) chocolate hazelnut
   spread

1 Preheat oven to 180°C/160°C fan-assisted. Grease oven trays; line with baking parchment.
2 Beat butter and sifted icing sugar in small bowl with electric mixer until light and fluffy. Stir in sifted dry ingredients.
3 Spoon mixture into piping bag fitted with 1cm-fluted tube. Pipe stars about 3cm apart on trays. Bake about 10 minutes; cool on trays. Sandwich biscuits with hazelnut spread.

makes 20

coffee meringue kisses

¾ cup (165g) caster sugar
1 teaspoon instant coffee granules
¼ cup (60ml) water
1 egg white
1 teaspoon malt vinegar
2 teaspoons cornflour
coffee butter cream
1 teaspoon instant coffee granules
2 teaspoons hot water
2 teaspoons coffee-flavoured
    liqueur
60g unsalted butter, softened
⅔ cup (110g) icing sugar

1 Preheat oven to 120°C/100°C fan-assisted. Grease four oven trays; line with baking parchment.
2 Combine sugar, coffee and the water in small saucepan; stir over heat until sugar is dissolved. Bring to a boil; remove pan from heat.
3 Meanwhile, combine egg white, vinegar and cornflour in small heatproof bowl; beat with electric mixer until foamy. With motor operating, add hot syrup to egg white in a thin, steady stream; beat about 10 minutes or until mixture is thick.
4 Spoon meringue into piping bag fitted with 5mm-fluted tube; pipe meringues, about 2.5cm in diameter, about 3cm apart, on trays. Bake about 30 minutes or until dry to touch. Cool on trays.
5 Meanwhile, make coffee butter cream. Sandwich meringues with butter cream just before serving.
coffee butter cream Dissolve coffee in the water; add liqueur. Beat butter and sifted icing sugar until light and fluffy; beat in coffee mixture.

makes 45

orange hazelnut butter yoyo bites

250g unsalted butter, softened
1 teaspoon vanilla extract
½ cup (80g) icing sugar
1½ cups (225g) plain flour
½ cup (75g) cornflour
orange hazelnut butter cream
80g unsalted butter, softened
2 teaspoons finely grated orange
  rind
⅔ cup (110g) icing sugar
1 tablespoon ground hazelnuts

1 Preheat oven to 160°C/140°C fan-assisted. Grease oven trays; line with baking parchment.
2 Beat butter, extract and sifted icing sugar in small bowl with electric mixer until light and fluffy; stir in sifted dry ingredients, in two batches.
3 Roll rounded teaspoons of mixture into balls; place about 3cm apart on trays. Using fork dusted with flour, press tines gently onto each biscuit to flatten slightly. Bake about 15 minutes; cool on trays.

4 Meanwhile, make orange hazelnut butter cream.
5 Sandwich biscuits with orange hazelnut butter cream; dust with extra sifted icing sugar, if desired.
orange hazelnut butter cream
Beat butter, rind and sifted icing sugar in small bowl with electric mixer until light and fluffy. Stir in ground hazelnuts.

makes 20

coffee hazelnut meringues

2 egg whites
½ cup (110g) caster sugar
2 teaspoons instant coffee granules
½ teaspoon hot water
3 teaspoons coffee-flavoured
  liqueur
¼ cup (35g) roasted hazelnuts

1 Preheat oven to 120°C/100°C fan-assisted. Grease oven trays; line with baking parchment.
2 Beat egg whites in small bowl with electric mixer until soft peaks form. Gradually add sugar, beating until dissolved between additions.
3 Meanwhile, dissolve coffee in the water in small jug; stir in liqueur. Fold coffee mixture into meringue.
4 Spoon mixture into piping bag fitted with 5mm fluted tube. Pipe meringues onto trays 2cm apart; top each meringue with a nut.
5 Bake about 45 minutes. Cool meringues in oven with door ajar.

makes 30

¾ cup (120g) sultanas
2 cups (80g) corn flakes
¾ cup (60g) roasted flaked
    almonds
½ cup (100g) red glacé cherries
⅔ cup (160ml) sweetened
    condensed milk
60g white eating chocolate, melted
60g dark eating chocolate, melted

1 Preheat oven to 180°C/160°C fan-assisted. Grease oven trays; line with baking parchment.
2 Combine sultanas, corn flakes, nuts, cherries and condensed milk in medium bowl.
3 Drop level tablespoons of mixture about 5cm apart on trays. Bake for 5 minutes; cool on trays.
4 Spread half the florentine bases with white chocolate; spread remaining half with dark chocolate. Run fork through chocolate to make waves; allow to set at room temperature.

makes 25

mini florentines

palmiers with honey cream

2 tablespoons raw sugar
1 sheet ready-rolled puff pastry
1 teaspoon ground nutmeg
300ml whipping cream
2 teaspoons honey

1 Preheat oven to 180°C/160°C fan-assisted. Grease two oven trays; line with baking parchment.
2 Sprinkle board lightly with a little of the sugar. Roll pastry on sugared board into 20cm x 40cm rectangle; trim edges. Sprinkle pastry with nutmeg and remaining sugar.
3 Starting from long side, loosely roll one side at a time into the middle of the rectangle, so the two long sides meet (see page 355).

4 Cut pastry rolls into 5mm-thick pieces. Place, cut-side up, about 5cm apart, on trays. Spread pastry open slightly at folded ends to make a V-shape.
5 Bake palmiers about 15 minutes or until golden brown; transfer to wire rack to cool.
6 Beat cream and honey in small bowl with electric mixer until firm peaks form. Serve palmiers with honey cream.

makes 30

pistachio & rosewater palmiers

¾ cup (110g) roasted shelled pistachios
¼ cup (55g) caster sugar
2 teaspoons rosewater
½ teaspoon ground cinnamon
20g butter, softened
2 tablespoons demerara sugar
2 sheets ready-rolled puff pastry, thawed
1 egg
½ cup (175g) honey
1 teaspoon rosewater, extra

1 Preheat oven to 200°C/180°C fan-assisted. Grease two oven trays.
2 Blend or process nuts, sugar, rosewater, cinnamon and butter until mixture forms a coarse paste.
3 Sprinkle board with half of the demerara sugar; place one sheet of pastry on the sugar. Using rolling pin, press pastry gently into demerara sugar. Spread half of the nut mixture on pastry
4 Fold two opposing sides of the pastry inwards to meet in the middle (see page 355). Flatten slightly; brush with a little egg. Fold the sides in half twice more so they touch in the middle, flattening slightly. Repeat process with

remaining ingredients. Wrap rolls, separately, in cling film; refrigerate 30 minutes.
4 Cut pastry rolls into 1cm slices; place slices, cut-side up, on trays about 1.5cm apart. Bake about 12 minutes or until palmiers are browned lightly both sides.
5 Meanwhile, combine honey and extra rosewater in small frying pan; bring to the boil. Reduce heat; simmer, uncovered, 3 minutes. Remove from heat. Add hot palmiers, one at a time, to honey mixture, turning to coat; drain on greased wire rack. Serve cold.

makes 32

pistachio almond crisps

3 egg whites
½ cup (110g) caster sugar
pinch ground cardamom
1 cup (150g) plain flour
½ cup (80g) blanched almonds
½ cup (70g) roasted unsalted
   pistachios

1 Preheat oven to 160°C/140°C fan-assisted. Grease 30cm-square piece of foil.

2 Beat egg whites in small bowl with electric mixer until soft peaks form. Gradually add sugar, beating until dissolved between additions. Transfer mixture to medium bowl.

3 Fold in sifted dry ingredients and nuts; spoon mixture onto foil, shape into 7cm x 25cm log. Enclose firmly in foil; place on oven tray.

4 Bake about 45 minutes or until firm. Turn log out of foil onto wire rack to cool.

5 Lower oven temperature to 120°C/100°C fan-assisted.

6 Using serrated knife, slice log thinly. Place slices close together in single layer on oven trays. Bake about 20 minutes or until crisp; transfer to wire racks to cool. Store in airtight container at room temperature for up to four weeks.

makes 65

maple-syrup butter whirls

125g butter, softened
½ teaspoon vanilla extract
⅓ cup (80ml) maple syrup
¾ cup (110g) plain flour
¼ cup (35g) cornflour

1 Preheat oven to 180°C/160°C fan-assisted. Grease oven trays; line with baking parchment.
2 Beat butter, extract and maple syrup in small bowl with electric mixer until light and fluffy; stir in combined sifted flours. Spoon mixture into piping bag fitted with 1cm fluted tube.
3 Pipe stars about 3cm apart onto trays. Bake about 15 minutes; cool cookies on trays.

makes 24

lemon shortbread whirls

250g butter, chopped
1 teaspoon finely grated lemon
  rind
⅓ cup (55g) icing sugar
1½ cups (225g) plain flour
½ cup (75g) cornflour
½ cup (85g) mixed peel, chopped
  finely

1 Preheat oven to 180°C/160°C fan-assisted.
2 Beat butter, rind and sifted icing sugar in small bowl with electric mixer until just changed in colour. Stir in sifted flours in two batches.
3 Place mixture into large piping bag fitted with fluted tube, pipe mixture into rosettes, about 2cm apart, onto lightly greased oven trays; sprinkle with mixed peel.
4 Bake about 15 minutes or until browned lightly. Stand on tray 10 minutes before transferring to wire rack to cool.

makes 40

macadamia shortbread

250g butter, chopped
½ cup (110g) caster sugar
2 teaspoons vanilla extract
2 cups (300g) plain flour
½ cup (75g) rice flour
½ cup (75g) finely chopped
   macadamias
2 tablespoons caster sugar, extra

1 Preheat oven to 170°C/150°C fan-assisted.
2 Beat butter, sugar and extract in small bowl with electric mixer until pale and fluffy. Transfer mixture to large bowl; stir in sifted flours and nuts in two batches. Press ingredients together. Turn onto lightly floured surface; knead until smooth (do not over knead).

3 Divide mixture into two portions. Roll each portion, between two sheets of baking parchment, into 23cm circle. Press an upturned 22cm loose-based fluted flan tin into shortbread to cut rounds. Cut each round into 12 wedges. Place on lightly greased oven trays; mark with a fork, sprinkle with extra sugar.
4 Bake about 20 minutes or until a pale straw colour. Stand on tray 10 minutes before transferring to wire rack to cool.

makes 24

nutty shortbread mounds

½ cup (75g) shelled pistachios
250g butter, chopped
1 cup (160g) icing sugar
1½ cups (225g) plain flour
2 tablespoons rice flour
2 tablespoons cornflour
¾ cup (90g) ground almonds
⅓ cup (55g) icing sugar, extra

1 Preheat oven to 150°C/130°C fan-assisted.
2 Toast nuts in small heavy-based frying pan until lightly browned; remove from pan. Coarsely chop ⅓ cup (50g) of the nuts; leave remaining nuts whole.
3 Beat butter and sifted icing sugar in small bowl with electric mixer until light and fluffy; transfer mixture to large bowl. Stir in sifted flours, ground almonds and chopped nuts.

4 Shape level tablespoons of mixture into mounds; place mounds on lightly greased oven trays, allowing 3cm between each mound. Press one reserved nut on each mound; bake about 25 minutes or until firm. Stand mounds on tray 5 minutes; transfer to wire rack to cool. Serve mounds dusted with extra sifted icing sugar.

makes 40

90g butter, softened
⅓ cup (75g) firmly packed brown
sugar
1 cup (150g) plain flour
icing sugar, for dusting
topping
1 cup (340g) mincemeat
2 eggs
½ cup (110g) firmly packed brown
sugar
2 tablespoons brandy
1 tablespoon self-raising flour
1½ cups (120g) desiccated coconut

1 Preheat oven to 180°C/160°C fan-assisted. Grease 20cm x 30cm baking tin; line with baking parchment, extending paper 5cm over long sides.
2 Beat butter and sugar in small bowl with electric mixer until pale in colour; stir in sifted flour, in two batches. Press dough over base of tin. Bake 10 minutes.
3 Meanwhile, make topping.
4 Press topping gently over base. Bake about 25 minutes or until slice is firm and golden brown. Cool slice in tin before cutting.

topping Blend or process mincemeat until chopped finely. Beat eggs, sugar and brandy in small bowl with electric mixer until thick and creamy; fold in flour, coconut and mincemeat.

makes 60

mincemeat bites

triple choc brownies

125g butter, chopped
200g dark eating chocolate,
  chopped
½ cup (110g) caster sugar
2 eggs
1¼ cups (185g) plain flour
150g white eating chocolate,
  chopped
100g milk eating chocolate,
  chopped

1 Preheat oven to 180°C/160°C
fan-assisted. Grease deep 19cm-
square cake tin; line base with
baking parchment, extending paper
5cm over sides.
2 Combine butter and dark chocolate
in medium saucepan; stir over low
heat until smooth. Cool 10 minutes.
3 Stir in sugar and eggs then sifted
flour and white and milk chocolates.
Spread mixture into tin. Bake about
35 minutes. Cool in tin.

makes 16

chocolate fudge brownies

150g butter, chopped
300g dark eating chocolate,
  chopped
1½ cups (330g) firmly packed
  brown sugar
3 eggs
1 teaspoon vanilla extract
¾ cup (110g) plain flour
¾ cup (140g) dark chocolate chips
½ cup (120g) soured cream
¾ cup (110g) roasted macadamias,
  chopped coarsely

1 Preheat oven to 180°C/160°C
fan-assisted. Grease 19cm x 29cm
rectangular slice tin; line base with
baking parchment, extending paper
5cm over sides.
2 Combine butter and chocolate
in medium saucepan; stir over low
heat until smooth. Cool 10 minutes.
3 Stir in sugar, eggs and extract
then sifted flour, chocolate chips,
soured cream and nuts. Spread
mixture into tin. Bake 40 minutes.
Cover tin with foil; bake a further 20
minutes. Cool in tin.
4 Dust brownies with sifted cocoa
powder, if desired.

makes 16

chocolate caramel slice

½ cup (75g) self-raising flour
½ cup (75g) plain flour
1 cup (80g) desiccated coconut
1 cup (220g) firmly packed brown
  sugar
125g butter, melted
395g can sweetened condensed
  milk
30g butter, extra
2 tablespoons golden syrup
200g dark eating chocolate,
  chopped coarsely
2 teaspoons vegetable oil

1 Preheat oven to 180°C/160°C fan-assisted. Grease 20cm x 30cm baking tin; line with baking parchment, extending paper 5cm over long sides.
2 Combine sifted flours, coconut, sugar and butter in medium bowl; press mixture evenly over base of tin. Bake about 15 minutes or until browned lightly.
3 Meanwhile, make caramel filling by combining condensed milk, extra butter and syrup in small saucepan. Stir over medium heat about 15 minutes or until caramel mixture is golden brown; pour over base. Bake 10 minutes; cool.
4 Make topping by combining chocolate and oil in small saucepan; stir over low heat until smooth. Pour warm topping over caramel. Refrigerate 3 hours or overnight.

makes 16

VARIATIONS
white chocolate topping Replace dark eating chocolate with 180g white eating chocolate.
mocha filling Dissolve 2 teaspoons instant coffee granules in 1 tablespoon hot water; add to the condensed milk mixture with 2 tablespoons coffee-flavoured liqueur. Cook as in step 3.

½ cup (75g) coarsely chopped
  raisins
2 tablespoons dark rum, warmed
150g milk eating chocolate,
  chopped coarsely
2 teaspoons vegetable oil
¼ cup (60ml) double cream
200g dark eating chocolate,
  chopped coarsely

1 Combine raisins and rum in small bowl. Cover; stand 3 hours or overnight.
2 Grease 8cm x 25cm slice tin; line base and two long sides with foil, extending foil 5cm over long sides.
3 Stir half of the milk chocolate and half of the oil in small heatproof bowl over small saucepan of simmering water until smooth; spread mixture over base of tin. Refrigerate about 10 minutes or until set.
4 Combine cream and dark chocolate in small saucepan; stir over low heat until smooth. Stir in raisin mixture, spread over chocolate base; refrigerate 20 minutes or until set.
5 Stir remaining milk chocolate and oil in small heatproof bowl over small saucepan of simmering water until smooth; spread over raisin mixture. Refrigerate about 40 minutes or until set; remove from pan before cutting.

makes 12

rum & raisin chocolate slice

choc-peppermint slice

250g digestive biscuits
100g butter, chopped
½ cup (125ml) sweetened
　condensed milk
70g peppermint crisp chocolate,
　chopped coarsely
chocolate topping
200g milk eating chocolate,
　chopped coarsely
2 teaspoons vegetable oil

1 Grease 19cm x 29cm slice tin; line base and two long sides with baking parchment, extending paper 2cm over long sides.
2 Process 200g of the biscuits until fine. Chop remaining biscuits coarsely.
3 Combine butter and milk in small saucepan; stir over low heat until smooth. Combine processed and chopped biscuits with chocolate bar in medium bowl; stir in butter mixture. Press mixture firmly into tin; refrigerate, covered, about 20 minutes or until set.
4 Meanwhile, stir ingredients for chocolate topping in small heatproof bowl over small saucepan of simmering water, until smooth; spread mixture over slice. Refrigerate until firm before cutting into 24 squares.

makes 24

VARIATIONS
lemon Replace peppermint crisp chocolate with 1 teaspoon finely grated lemon rind and 1 tablespoon lemon juice in the biscuit mixture. Press mixture firmly into tin; chill, covered, about 20 minutes or until set. Top with lemon icing made by stirring 1¼ cups (200g) icing sugar with 10g butter and one tablespoon lemon juice in small heatproof bowl over small saucepan of simmering water until smooth.
coffee & macadamia Replace peppermint crisp chocolate with ½ cup (70g) coarsely chopped roasted macadamias in the biscuit mixture. Press mixture firmly into tin; refrigerate, covered, about 20 minutes or until set. Top with icing made by dissolving 2 teaspoons instant coffee granules in 2 tablespoons boiling water in small heatproof bowl over small saucepan of simmering water; add 1¼ cups (200g) icing sugar and 10g butter, stirring until smooth.

top: lemon slice
bottom: coffee & macadamia slice
left: choc-peppermint slice

chocolate hazelnut slice

250g plain chocolate biscuits
60g butter, melted
4 eggs, separated
¾ cup (165g) caster sugar
½ cup (50g) ground hazelnuts
2 tablespoons plain flour
topping
125g butter, softened
½ cup (110g) caster sugar
1 tablespoon orange juice
200g dark eating chocolate,
   melted
1 tablespoon cocoa powder

1 Preheat oven to 180°C/160°C fan-assisted. Grease 20cm x 30cm baking tin; line base and two long sides with baking parchment, extending paper 2cm over long sides.
2 Process biscuits until fine. Combine one cup of the biscuit crumbs with butter in medium bowl; press over base of tin. Refrigerate 10 minutes.
3 Beat egg whites in small bowl with electric mixer until soft peaks form. Gradually add sugar, beating until dissolved between additions; fold in ground hazelnuts, remaining biscuit crumbs and flour.
4 Spread egg white mixture over biscuit base; bake 20 minutes. Cool 20 minutes. Reduce oven to 170°C/150°C fan-assisted.
5 Meanwhile, make topping by beating butter, sugar, egg yolks and juice in small bowl with electric mixer until light and fluffy. Stir in cooled chocolate.
6 Spread topping over slice; bake about 20 minutes, cool in tin. Refrigerate until firm; dust with sifted cocoa before cutting.

makes 24

date & lemon slice

1½ cups (225g) plain flour
1¼ cups (185g) self-raising flour
150g cold butter, chopped
1 tablespoon honey
1 egg
⅓ cup (80ml) milk, approximately
2 teaspoons milk, extra
1 tablespoon white sugar
date & lemon filling
3½ cups (500g) dried pitted dates,
    chopped coarsely
¾ cup (180ml) water
2 tablespoons finely grated lemon
    rind
2 tablespoons lemon juice

1 Grease 20cm x 30cm baking tin;
line base with baking parchment,
extending paper 5cm over long
sides.
2 Sift flours into large bowl; rub
in butter until mixture is crumbly.
Stir in combined honey and egg
and enough milk to make a firm
dough. Knead on floured surface
until smooth, cover; refrigerate
30 minutes.
3 Meanwhile, make date & lemon
filling.
4 Preheat oven to 200°C/180°C
fan-assisted.
5 Divide dough in half. Roll one half
large enough to cover base of tin;
press into tin, spread filling over
dough. Roll remaining dough large
enough to cover filling. Brush with
extra milk; sprinkle with sugar. Bake
about 20 minutes; cool in tin.

date & lemon filling Combine
ingredients in medium saucepan;
cook, stirring, about 10 minutes
or until thick and smooth. Cool to
room temperature.

makes 24

cherry almond coconut slice

60g butter, softened
⅓ cup (75g) caster sugar
1 egg yolk
2 tablespoons self-raising flour
½ cup (75g) plain flour
⅔ cup (220g) cherry jam
1 tablespoon cherry brandy
⅓ cup (25g) flaked almonds
coconut topping
2 eggs
¼ cup (55g) caster sugar
2 cups (160g) desiccated coconut

1 Preheat oven to 180°C/160°C fan-assisted. Grease 19cm x 29cm slice tin; line with baking parchment, extending paper 5cm over long sides.
2 Beat butter, sugar and egg yolk in small bowl with electric mixer until light and fluffy. Stir in sifted flours. Press mixture into tin; spread with combined jam and brandy.
3 Make coconut topping.

4 Sprinkle topping over slice, then sprinkle topping with nuts; press down gently.
5 Bake about 30 minutes; cool in tin before cutting.
coconut topping Beat eggs and sugar together with fork in medium bowl; stir in coconut.

makes 54

raspberry coconut slice

90g butter
½ cup (110g) caster sugar
1 egg
¼ cup (35g) self-raising flour
⅔ cup (100g) plain flour
1 tablespoon custard powder
⅔ cup (220g) raspberry jam
coconut topping
2 cups (160g) desiccated coconut
¼ cup (55g) caster sugar
2 eggs, beaten lightly

1 Preheat oven to 180°C/160°C fan-assisted. Grease 20cm x 30cm baking tin; line base with baking parchment, extending paper 5cm over long sides.
2 Beat butter, sugar and egg in small bowl with electric mixer until light and fluffy. Transfer to medium bowl; stir in sifted flours and custard powder. Spread dough into tin; spread with jam.

3 Make coconut topping; sprinkle topping over jam. Bake about 40 minutes; cool in tin.
coconut topping Combine ingredients in small bowl.

makes 16

choc-peanut caramel slice

125g butter, chopped
1 cup (220g) caster sugar
395g can sweetened condensed
   milk
1 cup (140g) roasted unsalted
   peanuts
200g dark eating chocolate
20g butter, extra

1 Grease deep 19cm-square cake tin. Fold 40cm piece of foil lengthways into thirds; place foil strip over base and up two sides of tin (this will help lift the slice out of the tin). Line base with baking parchment.
2 Combine butter, sugar and milk in medium heavy-based saucepan; stir over medium heat, without boiling, until sugar dissolves. Bring to a boil; boil, stirring constantly, about 10 minutes or until caramel mixture becomes a dark-honey colour and starts to come away from the base and side of pan.

3 Working quickly and carefully (the mixture is very hot), pour caramel into tin; smooth with metal spatula. Press nuts into caramel with spatula; cool 20 minutes.
4 Stir chocolate and extra butter in small heatproof bowl over small saucepan of simmering water until smooth; spread chocolate mixture over slice. Refrigerate until set. Use foil strip to lift slice from tin before cutting into squares.

makes 40

refrigerator biscuit slice

¾ cup (180ml) sweetened
   condensed milk
60g butter
125g dark eating chocolate,
   chopped coarsely
150g digestive biscuits
⅓ cup (45g) roasted unsalted
   peanuts
⅓ cup (55g) sultanas

1 Grease 8cm x 26cm slice tin; line base with baking parchment, extending paper 5cm over long sides.
2 Combine condensed milk and butter in small pan; stir over low heat until smooth. Remove from heat; add chocolate, stir until smooth.
3 Break biscuits into small pieces; place in large bowl with nuts and sultanas. Add chocolate mixture; stir to combine.
4 Spread mixture into tin, cover; chill about 4 hours or until firm. Remove from tin; cut into slices.

makes 12

small cakes & scones

There are so many variations on mini cakes, tiny bakes and scones – and its such a thrill to serve a plateful, all with different flavours and different decorations. Go the whole hog and dig out your best china, a doiley and some crisp napkins and make a proper afternoon tea. With very little effort, you can create the perfect lunch-box snack, cake stall winner or take-home gift for friends and family. We have lots of ideas for frostings, fillings and toppings – mix and match and choose your favourite!

orange syrup cakes

3 medium oranges (720g)
250g butter, chopped coarsely
1½ cups (330g) caster sugar
4 eggs
¾ cup (120g) semolina
¾ cup (90g) ground almonds
¾ cup (110g) self-raising flour
orange syrup
1 medium orange (240g)
½ cup (110g) caster sugar
1 cup (250ml) water

1 Preheat oven to 170°C/150°C fan-assisted. Line two 12-hole (80ml) muffin pans with paper cases.
2 Coarsely chop oranges, including skin; remove and discard seeds. Place oranges in medium saucepan, add enough boiling water to cover. Bring to a boil, simmer, uncovered, about 15 minutes or until tender; allow to cool.
3 Drain oranges, then blend or process until smooth.
4 Beat butter and sugar in small bowl with electric mixer until light and fluffy. Add eggs, one at a time, beating until just combined between additions.
5 Transfer mixture to large bowl; stir in semolina, ground almonds and sifted flour, then add orange puree. Spoon mixture into prepared cases.
6 Bake about 40 minutes.
7 Place hot cakes on wire rack over oven tray. Pour hot orange syrup over hot cakes. Serve warm or cold.

orange syrup Peel rind thinly from orange, avoiding any white pith. Cut rind into thin strips. Combine sugar and the water in small saucepan, stir over low heat, without boiling, until sugar is dissolved. Bring syrup to a boil; add rind, simmer, uncovered, 5 minutes. Transfer syrup to a heatproof jug.

makes 24

125g butter, softened
1 teaspoon vanilla extract
⅔ cup (150g) caster sugar
2 eggs
1¼ cups (185g) self-raising flour
½ cup (75g) plain flour
1 teaspoon mixed spice
½ teaspoon ground cinnamon
1 cup (250ml) buttermilk
1 large apple (200g), peeled,
   grated coarsely
caramelised apples
2 small apples (260g)
75g butter
⅓ cup (75g) firmly packed brown
   sugar

1 Make caramelised apples.
2 Preheat oven to 180°C/160°C fan-assisted. Grease two six-hole (180ml) large muffin pans with a little butter.
3 Place one slice caramelised apple in each pan hole; spoon caramel sauce over apple.
4 Beat butter, extract and sugar in small bowl with electric mixer until light and fluffy. Beat in eggs, one at a time. Transfer to large bowl; stir in sifted dry ingredients and buttermilk, in two batches. Stir in apple. Divide mixture among pan holes; bake about 30 minutes.
5 Stand cakes 5 minutes before turning, top-side up, onto wire rack. Serve cakes warm.
caramelised apples Slice each unpeeled apple into six 1cm-thick slices. Stir butter and sugar in large frying pan over low heat until sugar dissolves. Add apple slices to caramel sauce; cook, turning occasionally, about 3 minutes or until browned lightly.

makes 12

caramelised apple tea cakes

passionfruit curd sponge cakes

3 eggs
½ cup (110g) caster sugar
¾ cup (110g) self-raising flour
20g butter
¼ cup (60ml) boiling water
passionfruit curd
⅓ cup (80ml) passionfruit pulp
½ cup (110g) caster sugar
2 eggs, beaten lightly
125g unsalted butter, chopped
  coarsely

1 Make passionfruit curd.
2 Preheat oven to 180°C/160°C fan-assisted. Grease 12-hole (125ml) oval friand pan (see page xx) with softened butter; dust lightly with flour.
3 Beat eggs in small bowl with electric mixer until thick and creamy. Gradually add sugar, beating until dissolved between additions. Transfer mixture to large bowl. Fold in sifted flour then combined butter and the boiling water.
4 Divide mixture among pan holes. Bake about 12 minutes. Working quickly, loosen edges of cakes from pan using a small knife; turn immediately onto baking-parchment-covered wire racks to cool.
5 Split cooled cakes in half. Spread cut-sides with curd; replace tops. Serve lightly dusted with sifted icing sugar.

passionfruit curd Combine ingredients in medium heatproof bowl; stir over pan of simmering water about 10 minutes or until mixture coats the back of a wooden spoon. Cover; refrigerate 3 hours.

makes 12
tips You need four passionfruit to get the required amount of passionfruit pulp needed for this recipe. If you can't find the traditional oval friand pans, deep muffin pans will serve just as well.

250g butter, softened
1½ cups (330g) firmly packed dark
  brown sugar
3 eggs
¼ cup (90g) golden syrup
2 cups (300g) plain flour
1½ teaspoons bicarbonate of soda
2 tablespoons ground ginger
1 tablespoon ground cinnamon
1 cup (170g) coarsely grated apple
⅔ cup (160ml) hot water
lemon glacé icing
2 cups (320g) icing sugar
2 teaspoons butter, softened
⅓ cup (80ml) lemon juice

1 Preheat oven to 180°C/160°C fan-assisted. Grease two 6-hole mini fluted tube pans or large muffin pans.
2 Beat butter and sugar in small bowl with electric mixer until light and fluffy. Add eggs, one at a time, beat until well combined between additions. Stir in syrup.
3 Transfer mixture to medium bowl; stir in sifted dry ingredients, then apple and the water.
4 Divide mixture among prepared pans, smooth tops.
5 Bake about 25 minutes. Stand cakes in pan 5 minutes then turn onto wire racks to cool.
6 Meanwhile, make lemon glacé icing. Drizzle icing over cakes.

lemon glacé icing Sift icing sugar into medium heatproof bowl; stir in butter and juice to form a paste. Place bowl over small saucepan of simmering water; stir until icing is a pouring consistency.

makes 12
tip You will need one large apple (200g) for this recipe.

apple ginger cakes with lemon icing

mango & coconut jelly cakes

2 eggs
⅓ cup (75g) caster sugar
½ cup (75g) self-raising flour
2 teaspoons cornflour
10g butter
2 tablespoons boiling water
1 small mango (300g)
85g packet mango flavour jelly
  crystals
1¼ cups (310ml) boiling water,
  extra
1½ cups (115g) shredded coconut
300ml whipping cream

1 Preheat oven to 180°C/160°C fan-assisted. Grease 12-hole (25ml) muffin pan with a little butter.
2 Beat eggs in small bowl with electric mixer about 10 minutes or until thick and creamy; gradually add sugar, beating until dissolved between additions. Fold in sifted flours then combined butter and the boiling water.
3 Divide mixture among pan holes. Bake about 12 minutes. Turn cakes immediately onto baking-parchment-covered wire rack to cool.
4 Meanwhile, process half the mango until smooth (you need approximately ⅓ cup pulp). Combine jelly and the extra boiling water in large jug, stirring, until jelly dissolves; stir in mango pulp. Strain jelly into shallow dish; refrigerate until jelly is set to the consistency of unbeaten egg white.
5 Dip each cake into jelly then toss in coconut. Refrigerate 30 minutes.
6 Meanwhile, beat cream in small bowl with electric mixer until firm peaks form. Chop remaining mango finely; fold into cream. Cut cakes in half; sandwich with cream.

makes 12

VARIATION
raspberry & coconut jelly cakes
Omit mango jelly and replace with raspberry jelly. Omit fresh mango and replace with 300g fresh raspberries. Process half the berries until smooth, strain; discard seeds. Stir raspberry puree into jelly. Stir remaining raspberries into whipped cream.

strawberry powder puffs

2 eggs
⅓ cup (75g) caster sugar
2 tablespoons cornflour
2 tablespoons plain flour
2 tablespoons self-raising flour
½ cup (125ml) whipping cream
2 tablespoons icing sugar
½ cup (65g) finely chopped
   strawberries

1 Preheat oven to 180°C/160°C fan-assisted. Grease and flour three 12-hole shallow round-based patty tins.
2 Beat eggs and sugar in small bowl with electric mixer about four minutes or until thick and creamy.
3 Meanwhile, triple-sift flours; fold into egg mixture.
4 Drop 1 teaspoon of mixture into holes of tins. Bake about 7 minutes; turn immediately onto wire racks to cool. Wash, grease and flour tins again; continue using mixture until all puffs are baked.

5 Beat cream and half the sifted icing sugar in small bowl with electric mixer until firm peaks form; fold in strawberries.
6 Sandwich puffs with strawberry cream just before serving. Dust with remaining sifted icing sugar.

makes 36

ginger powder puffs with orange cream

2 eggs
⅓ cup (75g) caster sugar
2 tablespoons cornflour
1 tablespoon plain flour
2 tablespoons self-raising flour
1 teaspoon cocoa powder
1½ teaspoons ground ginger
¼ teaspoon ground cinnamon
orange cream
⅔ cup (160ml) whipping cream
2 tablespoons icing sugar
1 teaspoon finely grated orange
   rind

1 Preheat oven to 180°C/160°C fan-assisted. Grease and flour two 12-hole (1½ tablespoon/30ml) shallow round-based patty pans.

2 Beat eggs and sugar in small bowl with electric mixer until thick and creamy. Fold in triple-sifted dry ingredients. Divide mixture among pan holes. Bake about 8 minutes.
3 Working quickly, loosen edges of cakes using palette knife, then turn immediately onto baking-parchment-lined wire racks to cool.
4 Meanwhile, make orange cream: beat cream and sifted icing sugar in small bowl with electric mixer until firm peaks form; fold in rind.
5 Just before serving, sandwich puffs with orange cream. Serve lightly dusted with sifted icing sugar.

makes 12

rock cakes

2 cups (300g) self-raising flour
¼ teaspoon ground cinnamon
⅓ cup (75g) caster sugar
90g butter, chopped
1 cup (160g) sultanas
1 egg, beaten lightly
½ cup (125ml) milk
1 tablespoon caster sugar, extra

1 Preheat oven to 200°C/180°C fan-assisted. Grease oven trays.
2 Sift flour, cinnamon and sugar into medium bowl; rub in butter. Stir in sultanas, egg and milk. Do not over mix.
3 Drop rounded tablespoons of mixture about 5cm apart onto trays; sprinkle with extra sugar. Bake about 15 minutes; cool on trays.

makes 18

VARIATIONS

cranberry & fig Substitute caster sugar with ⅓ cup firmly packed brown sugar. Omit sultanas; stir 1 cup coarsely chopped dried figs and ¼ cup dried cranberries into mixture before egg and milk are added.

pineapple, lime & coconut Omit sultanas; stir 1 cup coarsely chopped dried pineapple, ¼ cup toasted flaked coconut and 1 teaspoon finely grated lime rind into mixture before egg and milk are added.

apricot & honey Omit sultanas; use half wholemeal self-raising flour and half white self-raising flour. Stir ½ cup (80g) finely chopped dried apricots and 2 tablespoons raisins into mixture before egg and milk are added; combine 2 tablespoons honey with the egg.

basic scones

4 cups (600g) self-raising flour
2 tablespoons icing sugar
60g butter
1½ cups (375ml) milk
¾ cup (180ml) water,
    approximately

1 Preheat oven to 220°C/ 200°C
fan-assisted. Grease 20cm x 30cm
baking tin.
2 Sift flour and sugar into large
bowl; rub in butter with fingertips.
3 Make a well in centre of flour
mixture; add milk and almost all
the water. Use knife to 'cut' the milk
and water through the flour mixture,
mixing to a soft, sticky dough.
Knead dough on floured surface
until smooth.
4 Press dough out to 2cm thickness.
Dip 4.5cm round cutter in flour; cut
as many rounds as you can from
piece of dough. Place scones, side
by side, just touching, in tin.
5 Gently knead scraps of dough
together; repeat pressing and
cutting of dough, place in same
tin. Brush tops with a little extra
milk; bake about 15 minutes or until
scones are just browned and sound
hollow when tapped firmly on the
top with fingers.

makes 20

VARIATIONS
sultana & lemon Add ½ cup
sultanas and 2 teaspoons finely
grated lemon rind to mixture after
butter has been rubbed in.
blueberry & ginger Add
3 teaspoons ground ginger and
½ cup fresh or frozen blueberries
to mixture after butter has been
rubbed in.

top: sultana & lemon
bottom: blueberry & ginger
right basic scones

spicy fruit tea scones

1¼ cups (310ml) hot strong
   strained black tea
¾ cup (135g) mixed dried fruit
3 cups (450g) self-raising flour
1 teaspoon ground cinnamon
1 teaspoon mixed spice
2 tablespoons caster sugar
20g butter
½ cup (120g) soured cream,
   approximately

1 Preheat oven to 220°C/200°C
fan-assisted. Grease 23cm-square
cake tin.
2 Combine tea and fruit in small
heatproof bowl, cover, let stand
20 minutes or until mixture is cooled
to room temperature.
3 Sift dry ingredients into large
bowl; rub in butter with fingertips.
Stir in fruit mixture and enough
soured cream to mix to a soft, sticky
dough. Knead dough on floured
surface until smooth.

4 Press dough out evenly to 2cm
thickness. Dip 5.5cm cutter into
flour; cut as many rounds as you
can from piece of dough. Place
scones side by side, just touching,
in tin. Gently knead scraps of dough
together; repeat pressing and
cutting out of dough, place in same
tin. Brush tops with a little milk.
5 Bake scones about 15 minutes or
until browned and scones sound
hollow when tapped firmly on the
top with fingers.

makes 16

buttermilk scones

2½ cups (375g) self-raising flour
1 tablespoon caster sugar
30g butter
1¼ cups (310ml) buttermilk,
   approximately

1 Preheat oven to 220°C/200°C
fan-assisted. Grease deep 19cm-
square cake tin.
2 Sift flour and sugar into large
bowl; rub in butter with fingertips.
3 Make well in centre of flour
mixture; add buttermilk. Using a
knife, 'cut' the buttermilk through
the flour mixture to mix to a soft,
sticky dough. Knead dough on
floured surface until smooth.

4 Press dough out to a 2cm
thickness. Dip 4.5cm cutter into
flour; cut as many rounds as you
can from the piece of dough. Place
scones side by side, just touching,
in tin. Gently knead scraps of dough
together; repeat pressing and
cutting of dough. Place in same tin.
Brush tops with a little extra milk.
5 Bake scones about 15 minutes
or until just browned and scones
sound hollow when tapped firmly
on the top with fingers.

makes 16

1 cup (160g) wholemeal self-raising
    flour
1 cup (150g) white self-raising flour
1 teaspoon ground cinnamon
½ cup (70g) fine oatmeal
½ teaspoon finely grated lemon
    rind
30g butter
¾ cup (105g) dried cranberries
1 cup (250ml) milk
2 tablespoons honey
1 tablespoon oatmeal, extra

1 Preheat oven to 220°C/200°C
fan-assisted. Grease and flour deep
19cm-square cake tin.
2 Sift flours and cinnamon into a
medium bowl, add oatmeal and
rind; rub in butter with fingertips.
Stir in cranberries.
3 Make a well in centre of flour
mixture; add combined milk and
honey. Using a knife, 'cut' the milk
and honey through the flour mixture
to mix to a soft, sticky dough.
Knead dough on floured surface
until smooth.
4 Press dough out to 2cm thickness.
Dip 5.5cm cutter into flour; cut as
many rounds as you can from the
piece of dough. Place scones side
by side, just touching, in tin. Gently
knead scraps of dough together;
repeat pressing and cutting of
dough. Place in same tin. Brush
tops with a little extra milk; sprinkle
with extra oatmeal.
5 Bake scones about 15 minutes or
until browned and scones sound
hollow when tapped firmly on the
top with fingers.

makes 12

cranberry, oatmeal
& cinnamon scones

almond friands

6 egg whites
185g butter, melted
1 cup (120g) ground almonds
1½ cups (240g) icing sugar
½ cup (75g) plain flour

1 Preheat oven to 200°C/180°C fan-assisted. Grease 12 x ½ cup (125ml) friand or muffin pans; place on oven tray.
2 Place egg whites in medium bowl; beat with a fork. Stir in butter, ground almonds and sifted icing sugar and flour until just combined.
3 Spoon mixture into pan holes.
4 Bake friands about 25 minutes. Stand in pans 5 minutes before turning, top-side up, onto wire rack. Serve dusted with extra sifted icing sugar, if you like.

makes 12

Friands are small densely-textured little sponge cakes, popular in Australia and New Zealand and similar to French Financiers. Traditionally baked in oval shapes, they gain their texture from the icing sugar and ground almonds that partly replaces the flour and they come in a variety of flavourings. If you can't find the traditional oval friand pans, deep muffin pans will serve just as well.

VARIATIONS
raspberry & white chocolate Stir 100g coarsely chopped white chocolate into egg-white mixture. Top friands with 100g fresh or frozen raspberries.
lime coconut Stir 2 teaspoons finely grated lime rind, 1 tablespoon lime juice and ¼ cup (20g) desiccated coconut into egg-white mixture; sprinkle unbaked friands with ⅓ cup (15g) flaked coconut.
passionfruit Use either almond or ground hazelnuts, then drizzle the pulp of 2 medium passionfruit over unbaked friands.
berry Top unbaked friands with 100g fresh or frozen mixed berries.
citrus & poppy seed Add 2 teaspoons grated lemon or orange rind and 1 tablespoon poppy seeds to egg-white mixture.
plum Use ground hazelnuts or ground almonds. Top unbaked friands with 2 medium (200g) thinly sliced plums.

top: almond
bottom: lime coconut
left: citrus & poppyseed

coffee & walnut friands

1¼ cups (125g) roasted walnuts
2 teaspoons instant coffee
  granules
2 teaspoons boiling water
6 egg whites
185g butter, melted
1½ cups (240g) icing sugar
½ cup (75g) plain flour
24 chocolate coated coffee beans

1 Preheat oven to 200°C/180°C fan-assisted. Grease 12-hole (125ml) muffin or oval friand pan.
2 Process nuts until ground finely.
3 Stir coffee and the water in small jug until dissolved.
4 Place egg whites in medium bowl; whisk lightly with fork until combined. Add butter, sifted icing sugar and flour, nuts and coffee mixture; stir until combined.

5 Divide mixture among pan holes; top each friand with two coffee beans. Bake about 20 minutes. Stand friands 5 minutes before turning, top-side up, onto wire rack to cool. Serve lightly dusted with sifted icing sugar.

makes 12

variation
coffee & hazelnut friands Omit the walnuts and replace with 125g ground hazelnuts.

coffee friands

6 egg whites
185g butter, melted
1 cup (125g) ground almonds
1½ cups (240g) icing sugar
½ cup (75g) plain flour
1½ tablespoons ground coffee
  beans

1 Preheat oven to 200°C/180°C fan-assisted. Grease 12-hole (125ml) muffin or oval friand pan.
2 Place egg whites in medium bowl; beat with a fork. Stir in butter, ground almonds, sifted icing sugar and flour, and coffee until combined. Spoon mixture into pan holes.
3 Bake friands about 20 minutes. Stand in pans 5 minutes before turning, top-side up, onto wire rack. Serve dusted with a little extra sifted icing sugar or cinnamon sugar, if you like.

makes 12

brandied cherry friands

1 cup (150g) frozen pitted cherries
2 tablespoons brandy
1 cup (120g) roasted pecans
6 egg whites
185g butter, melted
1½ cups (240g) icing sugar
½ cup (75g) plain flour
cherry sauce
¼ cup (55g) caster sugar
2 tablespoons water

1 Preheat oven to 200°C/180°C fan-assisted. Grease 12-hole (125ml) muffin or oval friand pan.
2 Combine cherries and brandy in small bowl; stand 30 minutes. Drain cherries; reserve liquid.
3 Process nuts until ground finely.
4 Place egg whites in medium bowl; whisk lightly with fork until combined. Add butter, sifted icing sugar and flour, and nuts. Divide mixture among pan holes; top with drained cherries. Bake about 20 minutes.

5 Meanwhile, make cherry sauce.
6 Stand friands 5 minutes before turning, top-side up, onto serving plates. Serve with cherry sauce.
cherry sauce Combine sugar, the water and reserved cherry juice in small saucepan; stir over low heat until sugar dissolves. Bring to the boil; reduce heat. Simmer, uncovered, about 3 minutes or until sauce thickens slightly.

makes 12

cherry friands

6 egg whites
185g butter, melted
1 cup (125g) ground almonds
1½ cups (240g) icing sugar
½ cup (75g) plain flour
250g fresh cherries, halved, pitted

1 Preheat oven to 200°C/180°C fan-assisted. Grease 12 x 125ml rectangular mini loaf tins or 12-hole (80ml) muffin pan; stand tins on oven tray.
2 Place egg whites in medium bowl; beat with a fork. Stir in butter, ground almonds and sifted icing sugar and flour until just combined. Spoon into tins; top with cherries.

3 Bake friands about 25 minutes. Stand in tins 5 minutes before turning, top-side up, onto wire rack.

makes 12
tips Cherries can be frozen for up to 18 months. Freeze them, in 250g batches, when they are in season. If you use frozen cherries, be sure to use them unthawed – this will minimise the 'bleeding' of colour into the mixture.

pineapple & coconut friands

6 egg whites
185g butter, melted
1 cup (120g) ground almonds
1½ cups (240g) icing sugar
⅓ cup (50g) plain flour
¾ cup (170g) finely chopped glacé
   pineapple
½ cup (40g) shredded coconut

1 Preheat oven to 200°C/180°C fan-assisted. Line 12-hole (125ml) muffin or oval friand pan with paper cases.
2 Place egg whites in medium bowl; whisk lightly with fork until combined. Add butter, ground almonds, sifted icing sugar and flour, pineapple and ⅓ cup of the coconut; stir until combined. Divide mixture among pan holes; sprinkle with remaining coconut. Bake about 20 minutes.
3 Stand friands 5 minutes before turning, top-side up, onto wire rack to cool.

makes 12
tips We used freeform paper cases made by pushing a 12cm square of paper (we used paper about the same thickness as printer paper) into ungreased pan holes, followed by a 12cm square of baking parchment.

VARIATION
peach & coconut friands Omit the glacé pineapple and replace with 150g finely chopped glacé peach.

lemon & coconut friands

6 egg whites
185g butter, melted
1 cup (100g) ground hazelnuts
1½ cups (240g) icing sugar
½ cup (75g) plain flour
2 teaspoons finely grated lemon
   rind
1 tablespoon lemon juice
¼ cup (20g) desiccated coconut
⅓ cup (15g) flaked coconut

1 Preheat oven to 200°C/180°C fan-assisted. Grease 12-hole (80ml) muffin pan.
2 Place egg whites in medium bowl; beat with fork. Stir in butter, ground hazelnuts, sifted icing sugar and flour, rind, juice and desiccated coconut until just combined.
3 Spoon mixture into pan holes; sprinkle with flaked coconut.
4 Bake friands about 20 minutes. Stand in pan 5 minutes before turning, top-side up, onto wire rack.

makes 12

choc-hazelnut friands

6 egg whites
185g butter, melted
1 cup (100g) ground hazelnuts
1½ cups (240g) icing sugar
½ cup (75g) plain flour
1 tablespoon cocoa powder
100g dark eating chocolate,
    chopped finely
¼ cup (35g) coarsely chopped,
    roasted hazelnuts

1 Preheat oven to 200°C/180°C fan-assisted. Line 12-hole (125ml) muffin or oval friand pan with paper cases.
2 Place egg whites in medium bowl; whisk lightly with fork until combined. Add butter, ground hazelnuts, sifted icing sugar, flour and cocoa, and chocolate; stir until combined.
3 Divide mixture among pan holes; sprinkle with nuts. Bake about 25 minutes. Stand friands 5 minutes before turning, top-side up, onto wire rack to cool.

makes 12

tips We used freeform paper cases made by pushing a 12cm square of paper (we used paper about the same thickness as printer paper) into ungreased pan holes, followed by a 12cm square of baking parchment.

VARIATION

choc-pecan friands Omit ground hazelnuts and replace with 100g finely ground pecans. Omit hazelnuts and replace with 35g coarsely chopped pecans.

pistachio & hazelnut friands

6 egg whites
185g butter, melted
¾ cup (75g) ground hazelnuts
¼ cup (35g) roasted shelled
    pistachios, chopped coarsely
1½ cups (240g) icing sugar
½ cup (75g) plain flour
2 teaspoons rosewater
⅓ cup (50g) roasted shelled
    pistachios, extra
toffee shards
⅔ cup (160ml) water
1⅓ cups (300g) caster sugar

1 Preheat oven to 200°C/180°C fan-assisted. Grease 8 x 125ml mini loaf tins; place on oven tray.
2 Place egg whites in medium bowl; beat with a fork. Stir in butter, ground hazelnuts, nuts, sugar, flour and rosewater until just combined. Spoon mixture into tins; top with extra nuts.
3 Bake friands about 30 minutes. Stand in tins 5 minutes before turning, top-side up, onto wire rack.
4 Meanwhile, make toffee shards.
5 Serve friands warm or at room temperature with toffee shards and thick cream, if you like.

toffee shards Stir ingredients in small saucepan over heat, without boiling, until sugar dissolves; bring to the boil. Reduce heat; simmer, uncovered, without stirring, about 10 minutes or until toffee is golden brown. Remove from heat; allow bubbles to subside. Pour hot toffee onto lightly oiled oven tray; do not scrape the toffee from pan, or it might crystallise. Allow toffee to set at room temperature; break into shards with hands.

makes 8

3 x 60g Mars Bars™
150g butter, chopped coarsely
150g dark eating chocolate,
    chopped coarsely
½ cup (110g) firmly packed brown
    sugar
1 cup (250ml) water
½ cup (75g) plain flour
¼ cup (35g) self-raising flour
2 eggs
chocolate fudge frosting
50g dark eating chocolate,
    chopped coarsely
25g butter
1 cup (160g) icing sugar
1 tablespoon cocoa powder
2 tablespoons hot water,
    approximately

1 Preheat oven to 180°C/160°C fan-assisted. Grease 12-hole (80ml) muffin pan.
2 Chop two Mars Bars™ finely; cut remaining bar into 12 slices.
3 Combine butter, chocolate, sugar and the water in medium saucepan; stir over low heat until smooth. Transfer to large bowl; cool 10 minutes. Whisk in sifted flours then eggs and finely chopped Mars Bars™.
4 Divide mixture into pan holes; bake about 25 minutes. Stand cakes in pan 5 minutes before turning, top-side up, onto wire rack to cool.
5 Meanwhile, make chocolate fudge frosting. Spread cakes with frosting; top each with a slice of Mars Bar™.

chocolate fudge frosting Stir chocolate and butter in small heatproof bowl over small saucepan of simmering water until smooth (do not allow water to touch base of bowl); stir in sifted icing sugar and cocoa. Stir in enough of the hot water until frosting is spreadable.

makes 12

chocolate fudge mud cakes

chocolate sticky date cakes

1¾ cups (250g) pitted dried dates
1⅓ cups (330ml) boiling water
1 teaspoon bicarbonate of soda
125g butter, softened
¾ cup (165g) firmly packed brown
  sugar
3 eggs
1½ cups (225g) self-raising flour
½ cup (95g) dark chocolate chips
chocolate icing
1½ cups (240g) icing sugar
1 tablespoon cocoa powder
50g butter, melted
2 tablespoons hot water,
  approximately

1 Preheat oven to 180°C/160°C fan-assisted. Grease 16 holes of two 12-hole (80ml) muffin pans.
2 Combine dates and the water in small saucepan; bring to the boil. Remove from heat; stir in bicarbonate of soda, stand 10 minutes. Blend or process mixture until almost smooth. Cool 10 minutes.
3 Beat butter and sugar in small bowl with electric mixer until light and fluffy. Beat in eggs, one at a time. Transfer mixture to large bowl; stir in sifted flour, chocolate and date mixture.
4 Divide mixture into pan holes; bake about 25 minutes. Stand cakes in pan 10 minutes before turning, top-side up, onto wire rack to cool.
5 Meanwhile, make chocolate icing. Spread cakes with icing.
chocolate icing Sift icing sugar and cocoa into small bowl; stir in butter and enough hot water to make icing spreadable.

makes 16

ginger cakes with orange glaze

⅔ cup (100g) plain flour
⅔ cup (100g) self-raising flour
½ teaspoon bicarbonate of soda
2 teaspoons ground cinnamon
2 teaspoons ground ginger
½ teaspoon ground cloves
1 cup (220g) firmly packed brown
  sugar
⅔ cup (160ml) buttermilk
2 eggs, beaten lightly
100g unsalted butter, melted
orange glaze
1 cup (160g) icing sugar
½ teaspoon finely grated orange
  rind
1 tablespoon strained orange juice
2 teaspoons hot water

1 Preheat oven to 180°C/160°C
fan-assisted. Grease and flour
8 holes of two 6-hole (180ml) mini
fluted tube pans.
2 Sift flours, soda, spices and sugar
into medium bowl, add buttermilk,
egg and butter; stir until smooth.
Divide mixture among pan holes;
bake about 30 minutes.
3 Turn cakes immediately onto
greased wire rack placed over tray.
Allow to cool.
4 Make orange glaze.
5 Pour glaze over cakes; stand until
glaze is set.
orange glaze Sift icing sugar
into medium bowl, add remaining
ingredients; stir until smooth.

makes 8

chocolate hazelnut cakes

100g dark eating chocolate,
chopped coarsely
¾ cup (180ml) water
100g butter, softened
1 cup (220g) firmly packed brown
  sugar
3 eggs
¼ cup (25g) cocoa powder
¾ cup (110g) self-raising flour
⅓ cup (35g) ground hazelnuts
whipped hazelnut ganache
⅓ cup (80ml) whipping cream
180g milk eating chocolate,
  chopped finely
2 tablespoons hazelnut-flavoured
  liqueur

1 Preheat oven to 180°C/160°C
fan-assisted. Grease twelve (½-cup/
125ml) large muffin pans.
2 Make whipped hazelnut ganache.
3 Meanwhile, combine chocolate
and the water in medium saucepan;
stir over low heat until smooth.
4 Beat butter and sugar in small
bowl with electric mixer until light
and fluffy. Add eggs, one at a
time, beating until just combined
between additions (mixture might
separate at this stage, but will come
together later); transfer mixture
to medium bowl. Stir in warm
chocolate mixture, sifted cocoa and
flour, and ground hazelnuts.
5 Divide mixture among pans; bake
about 20 minutes. Stand cakes
5 minutes; turn, top-sides up, onto
wire rack to cool. Spread ganache
over cakes.
whipped hazelnut ganache
Combine cream and chocolate in
small saucepan; stir over low heat
until smooth. Stir in liqueur; transfer
mixture to small bowl. Cover; stand
about 2 hours or until just firm. Beat
ganache in small bowl with electric
mixer until mixture changes to a
pale brown colour.

makes 12

125g butter, softened
1 teaspoon vanilla extract
¾ cup (165g) caster sugar
2 eggs
¾ cup (110g) self-raising flour
¼ cup (35g) plain flour
⅔ cup (80ml) apple juice
1 small red apple (130g)
1½ tablespoons demerara sugar
¼ teaspoon ground cinnamon

1 Preheat oven to 180°C/160°C fan-assisted. Grease 8-hole (125ml) mini loaf pan.
2 Beat butter, extract and sugar in small bowl with electric mixer until light and fluffy. Add eggs, one at a time, beating until just combined between additions.
3 Fold in combined sifted flours and juice in two batches. Spread mixture into prepared pan holes.
4 Cut the unpeeled apple into quarters; remove core, slice thinly. Overlap apple slices on top of cakes.
5 Combine demerara sugar and cinnamon in small bowl; sprinkle half the sugar mixture over cakes.
6 Bake about 25 minutes. Turn cakes onto wire rack to cool. Sprinkle with remaining sugar mixture.

makes 8
tip The cake mixture can also be cooked in large muffin pans.

buttery apple cinnamon cakes

mini sultana loaves

125g butter, melted
2⅓ cups (375g) sultanas
⅔ cup (150g) caster sugar
2 eggs
⅓ cup (80ml) buttermilk
½ cup (75g) plain flour
¾ cup (110g) self-raising flour
lemon glacé icing
1½ cups (240g) icing sugar
20g softened butter
2 tablespoons lemon juice,
    approximately

1 Preheat oven to 160°C/140°C fan-assisted. Grease 8-hole (180ml) mini loaf pan.
2 Stir ingredients in large bowl with wooden spoon until combined.
3 Divide mixture into pan holes, smooth tops; bake about 30 minutes. Stand cakes 5 minutes before turning, top-side up, onto wire rack to cool.
4 Meanwhile, make lemon glacé icing. Drizzle icing over cakes.

lemon glacé icing Sift icing sugar into small heatproof bowl; stir in butter and enough juice to make a firm paste. Stir over small saucepan of simmering water until icing is pourable.

makes 8

banana loaves with muesli topping

75g butter, softened
⅓ cup (75g) firmly packed brown
    sugar
1 egg
¾ cup (110g) self-raising flour
¼ teaspoon bicarbonate of soda
½ cup (115g) mashed over-ripe
    banana
¼ cup (60g) soured cream
1 tablespoon milk
¾ cup (75g) untoasted muesli
¼ cup (35g) dried cranberries

1 Preheat oven to 180°C/160°C fan-assisted. Grease six holes of 8-hole (180ml) mini loaf pan.
2 Beat butter and sugar in small bowl with electric mixer until light and fluffy. Beat in egg. Stir in sifted dry ingredients, banana, soured cream and milk.
3 Divide mixture between pan holes; sprinkle with combined muesli and cranberries. Bake about 25 minutes. Stand loaves in pan 5 minutes before turning, top-side up, onto wire rack to cool.

makes 6
tip You will need one large over-ripe banana (230g) for this recipe.

mini gingerbread loaves

200g butter, softened
1¼ cups (275g) caster sugar
¾ cup (270g) treacle
2 eggs
3 cups (450g) plain flour
1½ tablespoons ground ginger
3 teaspoons mixed spice
1 teaspoon bicarbonate of soda
¾ cup (180ml) milk
vanilla icing
3 cups (500g) icing sugar
2 teaspoons butter, softened
½ teaspoon vanilla extract
⅓ cup (80ml) milk

1 Preheat oven to 160°C/140°C fan-assisted. Grease two 8-hole (125ml) mini loaf pans or line 22 muffin pans (80ml) with paper cases.
2 Beat butter and sugar in small bowl with electric mixer until light and fluffy. Pour in treacle, beat 3 minutes. Add eggs one at a time, beating until just combined after each addition. Transfer mixture to large bowl. Stir in sifted dry ingredients, then milk. Divide mixture among prepared pans.
3 Bake about 25 minutes. Stand 5 minutes before turning onto wire rack to cool.
4 Spread icing over loaves; stand until set.
vanilla icing Sift icing sugar into heatproof bowl; stir in butter, vanilla and milk to form a smooth paste. Place bowl over simmering water; stir until icing is a spreadable consistency.

makes 16

rhubarb & almond cakes

½ cup (125ml) milk
¼ cup (40g) blanched almonds,
   toasted
80g butter, softened
1 teaspoon vanilla extract
½ cup (110g) caster sugar
2 eggs
1 cup (150g) self-raising flour
poached rhubarb
250g trimmed rhubarb, chopped
   coarsely
¼ cup (60ml) water
½ cup (110g) granulated sugar

1 Preheat oven to 180°C/160°C fan-assisted. Grease a 6-hole large (180ml) muffin pan.
2 Make poached rhubarb.
3 Meanwhile, blend or process milk and nuts until smooth.
4 Beat butter, extract and sugar in small bowl with electric mixer until light and fluffy. Add eggs, one at a time, beating until just combined between additions (mixture might separate at this stage, but will come together later); transfer to large bowl. Stir in sifted flour and almond mixture.
5 Spoon mixture equally among muffin pan holes; bake 10 minutes. Carefully remove pan from oven; divide drained rhubarb over muffins, bake further 15 minutes.
6 Stand muffins 5 minutes; turn, top-side up, onto wire rack to cool. Serve warm or cold drizzled with rhubarb syrup.

poached rhubarb Place ingredients in medium saucepan; bring to a boil. Reduce heat; simmer, uncovered, about 10 minutes or until rhubarb is just tender. Drain rhubarb over medium bowl; reserve rhubarb and syrup separately.

makes 6

2 eggs
⅓ cup (75g) caster sugar
2 tablespoons cornflour
2 tablespoons plain flour
2 tablespoons self-raising flour
200g milk eating chocolate
2 tablespoons icing sugar
nutty cream
½ cup (125ml) whipping cream
1 tablespoon icing sugar
1 tablespoon hazelnut-flavoured
  liqueur
2 tablespoons finely chopped
  roasted hazelnuts
2 tablespoons finely chopped
  roasted almonds

1 Preheat oven to 180°C/160°C fan-assisted. Grease and flour
3 x 12-hole shallow round-based patty pans.
2 Beat eggs in small bowl with electric mixer until thick and creamy. Gradually add caster sugar, beating until sugar dissolves between additions. Sift flours together three times; fold into egg mixture.
3 Drop rounded tablespoons of mixture into pan holes. Bake about 7 minutes; turn onto wire racks to cool.
4 Meanwhile, coarsely grate
1 tablespoon of chocolate from the 200g block; reserve grated chocolate. Melt remaining chocolate.
5 Make nutty cream.
6 Dip the knuckle of your index finger into icing sugar then use to make a large hollow in the flat side of the cakes.
7 Spoon 1 teaspoon of the nutty cream into each hollow; smooth level. Spread with melted chocolate. Set at room temperature.
8 Dust zucotto with sifted icing sugar to serve.

nutty cream Beat cream, sifted icing sugar and liqueur in small bowl with electric mixer until firm peaks form. Stir in nuts and reserved grated chocolate.

makes 36

choc-topped zucotto

florentine macaroons

1 egg white
¼ cup (55g) caster sugar
¾ cup (60g) shredded coconut
2 tablespoons finely chopped
  glacé apricots
2 tablespoons finely chopped
  glacé pineapple
2 tablespoons finely chopped
  glacé red cherries
2 tablespoons finely chopped
  glacé green cherries
2 tablespoons finely chopped
  unsalted, roasted pistachios

1 Preheat oven to 150°C/130°C fan-assisted. Line two 12-hole (1-tablespoon/20ml) mini muffin pans with paper cases.
2 Beat egg white in small bowl with electric mixer until soft peaks form; gradually add sugar, beating until dissolved between additions. Fold coconut and half the combined fruit and nuts into egg white mixture.
3 Divide mixture among paper cases. Sprinkle with remaining fruit and nut mixture. Bake macaroons about 20 minutes; cool in pans.

makes 24
tips Cover macaroons with foil halfway through baking time if fruit on top starts to brown. You need approximately 50g of each glacé fruit.

madeleines

2 eggs
2 tablespoons caster sugar
2 tablespoons icing sugar
¼ cup (35g) self-raising flour
¼ cup (35g) plain flour
75g unsalted butter, melted
1 tablespoon water
2 tablespoons icing sugar, extra

1 Preheat oven to 200°C/180°C fan-assisted. Grease two 12-hole (1½-tablespoons/30ml) madeleine pans.
2 Beat eggs and sifted sugars in small bowl with electric mixer until thick and creamy.
3 Meanwhile, triple-sift flours; sift flour over egg mixture. Pour combined butter and the water down side of bowl then fold ingredients together.
4 Drop rounded tablespoons of mixture into each pan hole. Bake about 10 minutes. Tap hot pan firmly on bench to release madeleines then turn, top-side down, onto wire rack to cool. Serve dusted with sifted extra icing sugar.

makes 24

VARIATION
orange madeleines Add 1 teaspoon finely grated orange rind when beating the egg mixture. Omit the water and replace with 1 tablespoon orange juice.

100g butter, softened
1 teaspoon orange flower water
½ cup (110g) caster sugar
2 eggs
1 cup (150g) self-raising flour
¼ cup (30g) ground almonds
½ cup (125ml) milk
orange blossom glacé icing
1 cup (160g) icing sugar
10g softened butter
1 teaspoon orange flower water
1 tablespoon water, approximately

1 Preheat oven to 180°C/160°C fan-assisted. Grease six-hole (180ml) mini fluted tube pan or large muffin pan.
2 Beat butter, orange flower water and sugar in small bowl with electric mixer until light and fluffy. Beat in eggs, one at a time (mixture will curdle). Stir in sifted flour, ground almonds and milk, in two batches.
3 Divide mixture into pan holes; bake about 25 minutes. Stand cakes in pan 5 minutes before turning, top-side up, onto wire rack to cool.
4 Meanwhile, make orange blossom glacé icing. Drizzle icing over cakes.
orange blossom glacé icing Sift icing sugar into small heatproof bowl; stir in butter, orange flower water and enough of the boiling water to make a firm paste. Stir over small saucepan of simmering water until icing is pourable.

makes 6

orange blossom cakes

large cakes

There is a special kind of satisfaction in turning out a good cake, and it's one that anyone can enjoy since cake-making is more a matter of care and attention than any special skill. Give yourself time to enjoy baking, and if you're liable to interruptions while you're cooking, try to make cakes when things are relatively quiet, or shift some of the preparation, such as preparing the tin and measuring ingredients, to an earlier quiet time. Then, when the time comes, you can give your full attention to the mixing and baking.

classic sponge cake

4 eggs
¾ cup (165g) caster sugar
⅔ cup (100g) cornflour
¼ cup (30g) custard powder
1 teaspoon cream of tartar
½ teaspoon bicarbonate of soda
⅓ cup (110g) apricot jam
300ml whipping cream, whipped

1 Preheat oven to 180°C/160°C fan-assisted. Grease and flour two deep 22cm-round cake tins.
2 Beat eggs and sugar in small bowl with electric mixer until thick, creamy and sugar dissolved; transfer to large bowl.

3 Fold in triple-sifted dry ingredients. Divide mixture between tins; bake about 20 minutes. Turn sponges, top-side up, onto baking-parchment-lined wire rack to cool.
4 Sandwich sponges with jam and cream.

serves 10

genoise sponge

4 eggs
½ cup (110g) caster sugar
⅔ cup (100g) plain flour
60g butter, melted
300ml whipping cream
1 tablespoon icing sugar
¼ cup (80g) strawberry jam, warmed
500g strawberries, sliced thinly
1 tablespoon icing sugar, extra

1 Preheat oven to 180°C/160°C fan-assisted. Grease deep 20cm-round cake tin; line base with baking parchment.
2 Place eggs and caster sugar in large heatproof bowl over large saucepan simmering water. Do not allow water to touch base of bowl. Beat with electric mixer until thick and creamy, about 10 minutes. Remove bowl from pan; beat mixture until it returns to room temperature.

3 Sift half of the triple-sifted flour over egg mixture, carefully fold in flour; fold in remaining sifted flour. Quickly and carefully fold in cooled butter. Pour mixture into tin.
4 Bake sponge about 20 minutes. Turn, top-side up, onto baking-parchment-covered wire rack to cool.
5 Beat cream and sifted icing sugar in small bowl with electric mixer until soft peaks form. Split sponge in half; place one half, cut-side up, on serving plate. Spread with jam and cream; top with strawberries, then remaining sponge half. Dust with extra sifted icing sugar and strawberries, if you like.

serves 8

4 eggs
¾ cup (165g) firmly packed dark
  brown sugar
1 cup (150g) cornflour
1 teaspoon cream of tartar
½ teaspoon bicarbonate of soda
300ml whipping cream
hazelnut praline
⅓ cup (75g) white sugar
¼ cup (60ml) water
½ teaspoon malt vinegar
⅓ cup (45g) roasted hazelnuts

1 Preheat oven to 180°C/160°C fan-assisted. Grease two deep 22cm-round cake tins.
2 Beat eggs and brown sugar in small bowl with electric mixer about 10 minutes or until thick and creamy; transfer to large bowl.
3 Sift cornflour, cream of tartar and soda twice onto paper then sift over egg mixture; gently fold dry ingredients into egg mixture. Divide mixture between tins; bake sponges about 18 minutes. Turn immediately onto baking-parchment-covered wire racks to cool.
4 Meanwhile, make hazelnut praline.
5 Beat cream in small bowl with electric mixer until firm peaks form; fold in praline. Place one sponge on serving plate; spread with half of the cream mixture. Top with remaining sponge; spread with remaining cream mixture.

hazelnut praline Stir sugar, the water and vinegar in small saucepan over heat, without boiling, until sugar dissolves; bring to a boil. Reduce heat; simmer, uncovered, without stirring, about 10 minutes or until syrup is golden brown. Add hazelnuts; pour praline mixture onto baking-parchment-covered tray. Cool about 15 minutes or until set. Break praline into pieces then blend or process until mixture is as fine (or coarse) as desired.

serves 10

brown sugar sponge

basic butter cake

250g butter, softened
1 teaspoon vanilla extract
1¼ cups (275g) caster sugar
3 eggs
2¼ cups (335g) self-raising flour
¾ cup (180ml) milk

1 Preheat oven to 180°C/160°C fan-assisted. Grease deep 22cm-round or 19cm-square cake tin; line with baking parchment.
2 Beat butter, extract and sugar in medium bowl with electric mixer until light and fluffy. Beat in eggs, one at a time. Stir in sifted flour and milk, in two batches.

3 Spread mixture into tin; bake about 1 hour. Stand cake 5 minutes; turn, top-side up, onto wire rack to cool.

serves 12

marble cake

1 quantity basic butter cake
   mixture (see recipe, above)
pink food colouring
2 tablespoons cocoa powder
2 tablespoons milk, extra
butter frosting
90g butter, softened
1 cup (160g) icing sugar
1 tablespoon milk

1 Follow steps 1 and 2 in basic butter cake recipe, above.
2 Divide mixture among three bowls; tint one mixture pink. Blend sifted cocoa with extra milk in cup; stir into second mixture. Drop alternate spoonfuls of mixtures into tin.
3 Pull a skewer backwards and forwards through cake mixture.
4 Bake cake about 1 hour. Stand cake 5 minutes; turn, top-side up, onto wire rack to cool. Top with butter frosting.
butter frosting Beat butter in small bowl with electric mixer until light and fluffy; beat in sifted icing sugar and milk, in two batches. Tint frosting pink with colouring.

serves 12

buttery orange cake

50g butter, softened
2 tablespoons finely grated orange
   rind
1½ cups (330g) caster sugar
4 eggs
1½ cups (225g) self-raising flour
½ cup (75g) plain flour
¾ cup (180ml) orange juice
orange glacé icing
1½ cups (240g) icing sugar
1 teaspoon soft butter
2 tablespoons orange juice

1 Preheat oven to 170°C/150°C fan-assisted. Grease deep 22cm-round cake tin; line base and side with baking parchment, bringing paper 5cm above edge of tin.
2 Beat butter, rind and sugar in large bowl with electric mixer until light and fluffy. Add eggs, one at a time, beating until just combined between additions. Fold in combined sifted flours and juice in two batches. Spread mixture into prepared tin.

3 Bake cake about 1 hour. Stand cake in tin 5 minutes before turning onto wire rack to cool.
4 Make orange glacé icing. Spread icing over top of cake.
orange glacé icing Sift icing sugar into small heatproof bowl; stir in butter and juice to form a firm paste. Place bowl over small saucepan of simmering water, stir until icing is a spreadable consistency; do not overheat.

serves 12

yogurt cake

125g butter, softened
1 cup (220g) caster sugar
3 eggs, separated
2 cups (300g) self-raising flour
½ teaspoon bicarbonate of soda
¼ cup (40g) finely chopped
   blanched almonds
1 cup (280g) plain Greek yogurt

1 Preheat oven to 180°C/160°C fan-assisted. Grease 20cm x 30cm baking tin; line base with baking parchment, extending paper 5cm over long sides.

2 Beat butter and sugar in small bowl with electric mixer until light and fluffy. Beat in egg yolks. Transfer mixture to large bowl; stir in sifted flour and soda in two batches. Stir in nuts and yogurt.
3 Beat egg whites in small bowl with electric mixer until soft peaks form. Fold egg whites into yogurt mixture, in two batches. Spread mixture into tin.
4 Bake cake about 35 minutes. Turn cake, top-side up, onto wire rack to cool. Dust with sifted icing sugar.

serves 12

pistachio buttercake with orange honey syrup

2 cups (280g) unsalted pistachios, chopped coarsely
185g butter, softened
1 tablespoon finely grated orange rind
¾ cup (165g) caster sugar
3 eggs
¼ cup (60ml) buttermilk
1½ cups (225g) self-raising flour
¾ cup (110g) plain flour

orange honey syrup
1 cup (220g) caster sugar
1 cup (250ml) water
1 tablespoon honey
1 cinnamon stick
1 teaspoon cardamom seeds
3 star anise
3 strips orange rind

1 Make orange honey syrup; cool.
2 Preheat oven to 180°C/160°C fan-assisted. Grease 23cm-square cake tin; line base and sides with baking parchment, extending paper 2cm over the sides. Sprinkle nuts evenly over base of tin.
3 Beat butter, rind and sugar in small bowl with electric mixer until light and fluffy. Add eggs, one at a time, beating until just combined between additions; transfer mixture to large bowl. Stir in combined buttermilk and ⅓ cup of the orange honey syrup, and sifted flours, in two batches.
4 Spread mixture into tin; bake about 40 minutes. Stand cake 5 minutes; turn, top-side up, onto baking-parchment-covered wire rack. Brush surface of hot cake with half of the remaining heated syrup.
5 Serve cake warm, drizzled with remaining heated syrup.

orange honey syrup Stir all ingredients in small saucepan over low heat, without boiling, until sugar dissolves; bring to a boil. Remove from heat; cool 15 minutes then strain.

serves 12

spiced teacake

60g butter, softened
1 teaspoon vanilla extract
½ cup (110g) caster sugar
1 egg
1 cup (150g) self-raising flour
⅓ cup (80ml) milk
20g butter, melted, extra
spiced nuts
2 tablespoons shelled pistachios, chopped finely
2 tablespoons blanched almonds, chopped finely
2 tablespoons pine nuts, chopped finely
¼ cup (40g) icing sugar
½ teaspoon ground allspice
½ teaspoon ground cardamom
1 teaspoon ground cinnamon

1 Preheat oven to 180°C/160°C fan-assisted. Grease 20cm-round cake tin.
2 Beat butter, extract, sugar and egg in small bowl with electric mixer until light and fluffy. Stir in sifted flour and milk.
3 Spread mixture into tin; bake about 25 minutes. Stand cake 5 minutes; turn, top-side up, onto wire rack to cool.
4 Meanwhile, make spiced nuts.
5 Brush cooled cake with extra butter; sprinkle with spiced nuts. Serve warm.

spiced nuts Place nuts in strainer; rinse under cold water. Combine wet nuts in large bowl with icing sugar and spices; spread mixture onto oven tray, toast in moderate oven about 10 minutes or until nuts are dry.

serves 12

madeira cake

180g butter, softened
2 teaspoons finely grated lemon rind
⅔ cup (150g) caster sugar
3 eggs
¾ cup (110g) plain flour
¾ cup (110g) self-raising flour
⅓ cup (55g) mixed peel
¼ cup (35g) slivered almonds

1 Preheat oven to 160°C/140°C fan-assisted. Grease deep 20cm-round cake tin; line base with paper.
2 Beat butter, rind and sugar in small bowl with electric mixer until light and fluffy; beat in eggs, one at a time. Transfer mixture to large bowl, stir in sifted flours.
3 Spread mixture into tin; bake 20 minutes. Remove from oven; sprinkle with peel and nuts. Return to oven; bake further 40 minutes. Stand cake 5 minutes; turn, top-side up, onto wire rack to cool.

serves 12

whipped cream cake with caramel frosting

600ml whipping cream
3 eggs
1 teaspoon vanilla extract
1¼ cups (275g) firmly packed
   brown sugar
2 cups (300g) self-raising flour
caramel frosting
60g butter
½ cup (110g) firmly packed brown
   sugar
2 tablespoons milk
½ cup (80g) icing sugar

1 Preheat oven to 180°C/160°C fan-assisted. Grease deep 22cm-round cake tin; line base with baking parchment.
2 Beat half of the cream in small bowl with electric mixer until soft peaks form. Beat eggs and extract in small bowl with electric mixer until thick and creamy; gradually add sugar, beating until dissolved between additions.
3 Transfer mixture to large bowl. Fold in a quarter of the whipped cream then sifted flour, then remaining whipped cream. Spread into tin; bake about 50 minutes. Stand cake 5 minutes; turn, top-side up, onto wire rack to cool.
4 Meanwhile, beat remaining cream in small bowl with electric mixer until firm peaks form.
5 Make caramel frosting.
6 Split cold cake in half; sandwich layers with cream. Spread cake with caramel frosting.

caramel frosting Melt butter in small saucepan, add brown sugar and milk; bring to a boil. Reduce heat immediately; simmer for 2 minutes. Allow to cool to room temperature. Stir in icing sugar until smooth.

serves 10

125g butter, softened
¾ cup (165g) firmly packed brown
  sugar
2 eggs
1½ cups (225g) self-raising flour
½ teaspoon bicarbonate of soda
1 teaspoon mixed spice
1 cup (230g) mashed banana
½ cup (120g) soured cream
¼ cup (60ml) milk
passionfruit icing
1½ cups (240g) icing sugar
1 teaspoon soft butter
2 tablespoons passionfruit pulp,
  approximately

1 Preheat oven to 180°C/160°C. Grease 15cm x 25cm loaf tin; line base with baking parchment.
2 Beat butter and sugar in small bowl with electric mixer until light and fluffy. Beat in eggs, one at a time. Transfer to large bowl; stir in sifted dry ingredients, banana, soured cream and milk.
3 Spread mixture into tin; bake about 50 minutes. Stand cake 5 minutes; turn, top-side up, onto wire rack to cool.
4 Meanwhile, make passionfruit icing. Spread cake with icing.
passionfruit icing Combine ingredients in medium bowl.

serves 10
tip You need approximately two large over-ripe bananas (460g) for this recipe as well as two large passionfruit.

banana cake with passionfruit icing

apple custard tea cake

200g butter, softened
½ cup (110g) caster sugar
2 eggs
1¼ cups (185g) self-raising flour
⅓ cup (40g) custard powder
2 medium green apples (300g),
    peeled, cored, sliced thinly
1 tablespoon butter, melted
2 teaspoons caster sugar, extra
½ teaspoon ground cinnamon
custard
2 tablespoons custard powder
¼ cup (55g) caster sugar
1 cup (250ml) milk
20g butter
2 teaspoons vanilla extract

1 Make custard.
2 Preheat oven to 180°C/160°C.
Grease deep 22cm-round cake tin;
line base with baking parchment.
3 Beat butter and sugar in small
bowl with electric mixer until light
and fluffy. Add eggs, one at a time,
beating well between additions. Stir
in sifted flour and custard powder.
4 Spread half the mixture into
prepared tin, top with custard. Top
custard with spoonfuls of remaining
cake mixture; gently spread with
spatula to completely cover custard.
Arrange apples on top; brush
with melted butter then sprinkle
with combined extra sugar and
cinnamon.
5 Bake cake 1¼ hours; cool in tin.
Sprinkle with extra caster sugar, if
desired.

custard Combine custard powder
and sugar in small saucepan;
gradually add milk, stirring over
heat until mixture thickens slightly.
Remove from heat; stir in butter and
extract. Press cling film over surface
of custard to prevent a skin forming;
cool. Whisk until smooth just before
using.

serves 8

almond honey spice cake

125g butter, softened
⅓ cup (75g) caster sugar
2 tablespoons honey
1 teaspoon ground ginger
1 teaspoon ground allspice
2 eggs
1½ cups (180g) ground almonds
½ cup (80g) semolina
1 teaspoon baking powder
¼ cup (60ml) milk
spiced syrup
1 cup (220g) caster sugar
1 cup (250ml) water
8 cardamom pods, bruised
2 cinnamon sticks
honey orange cream
¾ cup (180ml) whipping cream
1 tablespoon honey
2 tablespoons finely grated orange
    rind

1 Preheat oven to 180°C/160°C fan-assisted. Grease deep 20cm-round cake tin; line base and sides with baking parchment.
2 Beat butter, sugar, honey and spices in small bowl with electric mixer until light and fluffy. Add eggs, one at a time, beating until just combined between additions; transfer mixture to medium bowl. Fold in ground almonds, semolina, baking powder and milk.
3 Spread mixture into tin; bake about 40 minutes. Stand cake 5 minutes.
4 Meanwhile, make spiced syrup.
5 Pour strained hot syrup over hot cake in tin; cool cake in tin to room temperature. Turn cake, in tin, upside-down onto serving plate; refrigerate 3 hours or overnight.
6 Remove cake from refrigerator. Make honey orange cream. Remove tin from cake; serve cake at room temperature with honey orange cream.

spiced syrup Stir ingredients in small saucepan over heat, without boiling, until sugar dissolves; bring to a boil. Boil, uncovered, without stirring, about 5 minutes or until syrup thickens slightly.
honey orange cream Beat cream, honey and rind in small bowl with electric mixer until soft peaks form.

serves 10

lemon cake

125g butter, softened
2 teaspoons finely grated lemon rind
1¼ cups (275g) caster sugar
3 eggs
1½ cups (225g) self-raising flour
½ cup (125ml) milk
¼ cup (60ml) lemon juice
lemon marscapone frosting
300ml whipping cream
½ cup icing sugar
2 teaspoons finely grated lemon rind
150g mascarpone

1 Preheat oven to 180°C/160°C fan-assisted. Grease deep 20cm-round cake tin; line base with baking parchment.
2 Make lemon mascarpone frosting. Refrigerate, covered, until required.
3 Beat butter, rind and sugar in small bowl with electric mixer until light and fluffy. Add eggs, one at a time, beating until just combined between additions (mixture might separate at this stage, but will come together later); transfer mixture to large bowl. Stir in sifted flour, milk and juice, in two batches.

4 Pour mixture into tin; bake about 50 minutes. Stand cake 5 minutes; turn, top-side up, onto wire rack to cool.
5 Split cold cake into three layers, place one layer onto serving plate, cut-side up; spread with one-third of the frosting. Repeat layering process, finishing with frosting.
lemon marscapone frosting Beat cream, sifted icing sugar and rind in small bowl with electric mixer until soft peaks form. Fold cream mixture into mascarpone.

serves 12

orange cake

150g butter, softened
1 tablespoon finely grated orange rind
⅔ cup (150g) caster sugar
3 eggs
1½ cups (225g) self-raising flour
¼ cup (60ml) milk
¾ cup (120g) icing sugar
1½ tablespoons orange juice

1 Preheat oven to 180°C/160°C fan-assisted. Grease deep 20cm-round cake tin.
2 Beat butter, rind, caster sugar, eggs, flour and milk in medium bowl with electric mixer at low speed until just combined. Increase speed to medium, beat about 3 minutes or until mixture is smooth.
3 Spread mixture into tin; bake about 40 minutes. Stand cake 5 minutes; turn, top-side up, onto wire rack to cool.
4 Combine sifted icing sugar and juice in small bowl; spread over cake.

serves 12

185g butter, softened
½ cup (110g) caster sugar
3 eggs
1½ cups (185g) ground almonds
¼ cup (35g) plain flour
420g can pear halves in natural
    juice, drained
passionfruit glaze
⅓ cup (80ml) passionfruit pulp
⅓ cup (80ml) light corn syrup
1 tablespoon caster sugar

1 Preheat oven to 170°C/150°C fan-assisted. Grease 22cm springform tin; line base and sides with baking parchment.
2 Beat butter and sugar in medium bowl with electric mixer until light and fluffy. Add eggs, one at a time, beating until combined between each addition. Stir in ground almonds and flour. Spread mixture into prepared tin; top with pear halves, cut-side down.
3 Bake cake about 50 minutes. Stand cake in tin 5 minutes before transferring to a serving plate. Pour passionfruit glaze over cake while still warm.
passionfruit glaze Stir combined ingredients in small saucepan over heat, without boiling, until sugar dissolves. Bring to a boil; reduce heat. Simmer, uncovered, without stirring, about 2 minutes or until thickened slightly; cool.

serves 10
tips You will need about four passionfruit for this recipe. Cake can be made a day ahead; keep, covered, in the refrigerator until required. Cover cake with glaze on day of serving. Bring glaze to room temperature before using.

pear & almond cake with passionfruit glaze

coconut cake

125g butter, softened
½ teaspoon coconut essence
1 cup (220g) caster sugar
2 eggs
½ cup (40g) desiccated coconut
1½ cups (225g) self-raising flour
1¼ cups (300g) soured cream
⅓ cup (80ml) milk
coconut ice frosting
2 cups (320g) icing sugar
1⅓ cups (100g) desiccated coconut
2 egg whites, beaten lightly
pink food colouring

1 Preheat oven to 180°C/160°C fan-assisted. Grease deep 23cm-square cake pan; line with baking parchment.
2 Beat butter, essence and sugar in small bowl with electric mixer until light and fluffy. Beat in eggs, one at a time. Transfer mixture to large bowl; stir in coconut, sifted flour, soured cream and milk, in two batches.
3 Spread mixture into tin; bake about 40 minutes. Stand cake 5 minutes; turn, top-side up, onto wire rack to cool.

4 Meanwhile, make coconut ice frosting. Drop alternate spoonfuls of white and pink frosting onto cake; marble over top of cake.
coconut ice frosting Sift icing sugar into medium bowl; stir in coconut and egg white. Place half the mixture in small bowl; tint with pink colouring.

serves 16

pineapple coconut cake

185g butter, softened
¾ cup (165g) caster sugar
3 eggs
⅔ cup (50g) desiccated coconut
1¾ cups (260g) self-raising flour
270ml can coconut cream
440g can crushed pineapple,
    well-drained
⅓ cup (25g) shredded coconut
lime glacé icing
1½ cups (240g) icing sugar
20g butter, melted
2 tablespoons lime juice,
    approximately

1 Preheat oven to 180°C/160°C fan-assisted. Grease 22cm x 32cm rectangular cake tin; line base and sides with baking parchment, extending paper 5cm over edges.
2 Beat butter and sugar in small bowl with electric mixer until light and fluffy. Beat in eggs, one at a time. Transfer mixture to large bowl; stir in coconut, sifted flour, coconut cream and pineapple, in two batches.
3 Spread mixture into tin; bake 45 minutes. Stand cake in tin 10 minutes before turning, top-side up, onto wire rack to cool.

4 Meanwhile, make lime glacé icing; spread icing over cake, sprinkle with coconut.
lime glacé icing Sift icing sugar into small heatproof bowl; stir in butter and enough of the juice to make a soft paste. Stir over small saucepan of simmering water until icing is spreadable.

serves 20

apple streusel cake

200g butter, softened
2 teaspoons finely grated
   lemon rind
⅔ cup (150g) caster sugar
3 eggs
1 cup (150g) self-raising flour
½ cup (75g) plain flour
⅓ cup (80ml) milk
5 medium apples (750g)
25g butter, extra
⅓ cup (75g) firmly packed
   brown sugar
streusel topping
½ cup (75g) plain flour
¼ cup (35g) self-raising flour
⅓ cup (75g) firmly packed
   brown sugar
½ teaspoon ground cinnamon
80g butter, chopped finely

1 Preheat oven to 180°C/160°C fan-assisted. Grease deep 23cm-round cake tin; line with baking parchment.
2 Make streusel topping.
3 Beat butter, rind and caster sugar in small bowl with electric mixer until light and fluffy. Beat in eggs, one at a time. Transfer to large bowl; stir in sifted flours and milk, in two batches. Spread mixture into tin; bake 25 minutes.
4 Meanwhile, peel, core and quarter apples; slice thinly. Melt extra butter in large frying pan; cook apple, stirring, about 5 minutes or until browned lightly. Add brown sugar; cook, stirring, about 5 minutes or until mixture thickens slightly. Set aside.
5 Remove cake from oven. Working quickly, top cake with apple mixture; coarsely grate streusel over apple. Return to oven; bake about 25 minutes. Stand cake 10 minutes; turn, top-side up, onto wire rack to cool. Serve cake warm or cold.

streusel topping Process flours, sugar and cinnamon until combined. Add butter; process until ingredients just come together. Wrap in cling film; freeze about 1 hour or until firm.

serves 16

500g butter, softened
3 cups (660g) caster sugar
8 eggs
2 cups (300g) plain flour
1½ cups (225g) self-raising flour
1 cup (125g) ground almonds
1 cup (250ml) milk
1 cup (140g) slivered almonds, toasted, chopped finely
400g fresh or frozen raspberries
400g caramelised almonds
mascarpone cream
750g mascarpone
300g soured cream
1 cup (160g) icing sugar
⅓ cup (80ml) orange-flavoured liqueur

1 Preheat oven to 170°C/150°C fan-assisted. Grease deep 30cm-round cake tin; line base and sides with two layers of baking parchment, extending 5cm above edge of tin.
2 Beat butter and sugar in large bowl with electric mixer until light and fluffy. Add eggs one at a time, beating until just combined between additions (the mixture may appear curdled at this stage).
3 Transfer mixture to very large bowl; fold in sifted flours, ground almonds and milk in three batches. Fold in chopped almonds and raspberries, then spread mixture into prepared tin.
4 Bake cake 1 hour, then reduce oven temperature to 150°C/130°C fan-assisted and bake about 1 hour. Stand in tin 20 minutes before turning cake onto wire rack to cool.
5 Using large serrated knife, split cake into three layers. Place base layer on serving plate; spread with a third of the mascarpone cream, repeat layering, ending with mascarpone cream. Decorate top of cake with caramelised almonds.

mascarpone cream Beat mascarpone, soured cream and icing sugar in large bowl with electric mixer until soft peaks form; stir in liqueur.

serves 25

raspberry & almond mascarpone cake

passionfruit & lemon syrup cake

⅔ cup (160ml) passionfruit pulp
250g butter, softened
1 tablespoon finely grated lemon
    rind
1 cup (220g) caster sugar
3 eggs
1 cup (250ml) buttermilk
2 cups (300g) self-raising flour
lemon syrup
⅓ cup (80ml) lemon juice
¼ cup (60ml) water
¾ cup (165g) caster sugar

1 Preheat oven to 180°C/160°C fan-assisted. Grease deep 19cm-square cake tin; line base and sides with baking parchment.
2 Strain passionfruit over medium jug; reserve both juice and seeds.
3 Beat butter, rind and sugar in small bowl with electric mixer until light and fluffy. Add eggs, one at a time, beating until combined between additions; transfer to large bowl.
4 Fold in combined passionfruit juice and buttermilk, and sifted flour, in two batches. Spread mixture into tin; bake about 1 hour.
5 Meanwhile, make lemon syrup.
6 Stand cake 5 minutes; turn, top-side up, onto wire rack set over tray. Pour hot syrup over hot cake; serve warm.
lemon syrup Combine juice, the water, sugar and half of the reserved passionfruit seeds (discard remaining seeds or freeze for future use) in small saucepan; stir over heat, without boiling, until sugar dissolves. Simmer, uncovered, without stirring, 5 minutes.

serves 16

lemon sour cream cake

250g butter, softened
1 tablespoon finely grated
  lemon rind
2 cups (440g) caster sugar
6 eggs
¾ cup (180g) soured cream
2 cups (300g) plain flour
¼ cup (35g) self-raising flour
½ cup (80g) pine nuts
1 tablespoon demerara sugar
¼ cup (90g) honey

1 Preheat oven to 170°C/150°C fan-assisted. Grease deep 23cm-square cake tin; line base and two opposite sides with baking parchment, extending paper 5cm over sides.
2 Beat butter, rind and caster sugar in medium bowl with electric mixer until light and fluffy. Add eggs, one at a time, beating until just combined between additions (mixture might separate at this stage, but will come together later). Stir in soured cream and sifted flours, in two batches. Spread mixture into tin; bake 15 minutes.

3 Meanwhile, combine pine nuts and demerara sugar in small bowl.
4 Carefully remove cake from oven; working quickly, sprinkle evenly with nut mixture, press gently into cake. Return cake to oven; bake further 45 minutes. Stand cake 5 minutes; turn, top-side up, onto wire rack.
5 Meanwhile, heat honey in small saucepan. Drizzle hot cake evenly with hot honey; cool before serving.

serves 16

orange, almond & pine nut cake

2 medium oranges (480g)
1 teaspoon baking powder
6 eggs
1 cup (220g) caster sugar
2 cups (240g) ground almonds
½ cup (75g) plain flour
⅓ cup (50g) pine nuts

1 Place unpeeled whole oranges in medium saucepan, cover with cold water; bring to the boil. Boil, covered, 1½ hours or until oranges are tender; drain. Cool.
2 Preheat oven to 180°C/160°C fan-assisted. Grease deep 23cm-round cake tin; line base and sides with baking parchment.

3 Trim and discard ends from oranges. Halve oranges; discard seeds. Blend or process oranges, including rind, with baking powder until mixture is pulpy.
4 Beat eggs and sugar in medium bowl with electric mixer about 5 minutes or until thick and creamy. Fold in ground almonds, sifted flour and orange pulp.
5 Pour mixture into tin, sprinkle with nuts; bake about 1 hour. Cool cake in tin.

serves 16

mandarin, polenta & macadamia cake

4 small mandarins (400g),
  unpeeled
2 cups (280g) macadamias
250g butter, softened
1 teaspoon vanilla extract
1 cup (220g) caster sugar
3 eggs
1 cup (170g) polenta
1 teaspoon baking powder
1 tablespoon icing sugar

1 Cover whole mandarins in medium saucepan with cold water; bring to a boil. Drain then repeat process two more times. Cool mandarins to room temperature.
2 Preheat oven to 170°C/150°C fan-assisted. Grease deep 22cm-round cake tin; line base with baking parchment.
3 Blend or process nuts until mixture forms a coarse flour. Halve mandarins; discard seeds. Blend or process mandarins until pulpy.
4 Beat butter, extract and caster sugar in small bowl with electric mixer until light and fluffy. Add eggs, one at a time, beating until just combined between additions; transfer to large bowl. Stir in polenta, baking powder, ground nuts and mandarin pulp.
5 Spread mixture into tin; bake about 1 hour. Stand cake 15 minutes; turn, top-side up, onto wire rack to cool. Serve cake dusted with sifted icing sugar.

serves 10

plum & hazelnut upside-down cake

50g butter, chopped
½ cup (110g) firmly packed brown
  sugar
6 medium plums (680g), halved,
  stones removed
185g butter, softened, extra
1 cup (220g) firmly packed brown
  sugar, extra
3 eggs
½ cup (50g) ground hazelnuts
½ cup (75g) self-raising flour
½ cup (75g) plain flour

1 Preheat oven to 180°C/160°C fan-assisted. Grease deep 22cm-round cake tin; line base with baking parchment.
2 Combine butter and sugar in small saucepan, stir over low heat until smooth; pour over cake tin base. Place plums, cut side down, over tin base.
3 Beat extra butter and extra sugar in small bowl with electric mixer until creamy. Add eggs, one at a time, beating until combined between additions; transfer mixture to large bowl.
4 Stir in ground hazelnuts and sifted flours; spread mixture into prepared tin.
5 Bake cake in moderate oven about 1 hour. Stand cake in tin 5 minutes before turning onto serving plate.

serves 8

fresh ginger cake with golden ginger cream

250g butter, chopped
½ cup (110g) firmly packed brown sugar
⅔ cup (230g) golden syrup
12cm piece fresh ginger (60g), grated finely
1 cup (150g) plain flour
1 cup (150g) self-raising flour
½ teaspoon bicarbonate of soda
2 eggs, beaten lightly
¾ cup (180ml) whipping cream
golden ginger cream
300ml whipping cream
2 tablespoons golden syrup
2 teaspoons ground ginger

1 Preheat oven to 180°C/160°C fan-assisted. Grease deep 22cm-round cake tin.
2 Melt butter in medium saucepan; add sugar, syrup and ginger. Stir over low heat until sugar dissolves.
3 Whisk in combined sifted flours and soda then eggs and cream. Pour mixture into tin; bake about 50 minutes. Stand cake 10 minutes before turning, top-side up, onto wire rack to cool.

4 Meanwhile, beat golden ginger cream ingredients in small bowl with electric mixer until soft peaks form. Serve cake with cream.

serves 8

lemon iced gingerbread

1 cup (350g) golden syrup
1 cup (250ml) water
⅔ cup (150g) firmly packed brown sugar
250g butter, chopped
3½ cups (525g) plain flour
1 teaspoon bicarbonate of soda
2 tablespoons ground ginger
1 teaspoon ground nutmeg
1 teaspoon ground cinnamon
lemon icing
60g butter, softened
2 teaspoons finely grated lemon rind
2 tablespoons lemon juice
2 cups (320g) icing sugar

1 Preheat oven to 160°C/140°C fan-assisted. Grease 23cm-square cake tin; line base with baking parchment, extending paper 5cm over sides.
2 Combine syrup, the water, sugar and butter in large saucepan; stir over low heat until smooth. Bring to a boil; remove from heat, cool to room temperature. Stir in sifted dry ingredients.
3 Pour mixture into tin; bake about 1 hour. Stand cake 5 minutes; turn, top-side up, onto wire rack to cool.
4 Meanwhile, make lemon icing. Spread cake with icing.

lemon icing Beat butter and rind in small bowl until smooth; gradually stir in juice and sifted icing sugar.

serves 16

217

chocoholic's chocolate cake

250g butter, chopped
1 tablespoon instant coffee
   granules
1½ cups (375ml) water
2 cups (440g) caster sugar
1 teaspoon vanilla extract
200g dark eating chocolate,
   chopped coarsely
2 eggs, beaten lightly
1½ cups (225g) self-raising flour
1 cup (150g) plain flour
¼ cup (25g) cocoa powder
⅓ cup (80ml) double cream
180g white eating chocolate,
   melted
2 x 45g packets Maltesers™

1 Preheat oven to 150°C/130°C fan-assisted. Grease deep 19cm-square cake tin; line base and sides with baking parchment.
2 Heat butter, coffee, the water, sugar, extract and half of the dark chocolate in large saucepan, stirring until smooth. Transfer to large bowl; cool 20 minutes. Stir in eggs and sifted dry ingredients.
3 Pour mixture into tin; bake about 1 hour 50 minutes. Stand cake 15 minutes; turn, top-side up, onto wire rack to cool.
4 Combine cream and remaining dark chocolate in small saucepan, stirring over low heat until ganache mixture is smooth. Cover; refrigerate 1 hour or until ganache is firm.
5 Spread white chocolate into 15cm x 20cm rectangle onto baking parchment; stand until just set. Using 3cm- and 5cm-star cutter, cut as many stars as possible from white chocolate. Stand about 30 minutes or until firm.
6 Spread cake with ganache; decorate with stars and Maltesers™.

chocolate cake

125g butter, softened
1 teaspoon vanilla extract
1¼ cups (275g) caster sugar
2 eggs
1⅓ cups (200g) self-raising flour
½ cup (50g) cocoa powder
⅔ cup (160ml) water
chocolate icing
90g dark eating chocolate,
  chopped coarsely
30g butter
1 cup (160g) icing sugar
2 tablespoons hot water

1 Preheat oven to 180°C/160°C fan-assisted. Grease deep 20cm-round cake tin; line with baking parchment.
2 Beat butter, extract, sugar, eggs, sifted flour and cocoa, and the water in large bowl with electric mixer on low speed until ingredients are combined. Increase speed to medium; beat about 3 minutes or until mixture is smooth and paler in colour.
3 Spread mixture into tin; bake about 1 hour. Stand cake 5 minutes; turn, top-side up, onto wire rack to cool.

4 Meanwhile, make chocolate icing. Spread cake with icing.
chocolate icing Melt chocolate and butter in small heatproof bowl over small saucepan of simmering water; gradually stir in sifted icing sugar and the hot water, stirring until icing is spreadable.

serves 20

low-fat chocolate cake

½ cup (160g) plum jam
½ cup (110g) firmly packed
  brown sugar
½ cup (50g) cocoa powder
¾ cup (180ml) low-fat evaporated
  milk
2 teaspoons instant coffee
  granules
50g butter
2 eggs
½ cup (110g) caster sugar
1 cup (150g) self-raising flour
⅓ cup (50g) plain flour
2 teaspoons icing sugar

1 Preheat oven to 180°C/160°C fan-assisted. Spray 21cm baba cake tin with cooking-oil spray.
2 Combine jam, brown sugar, sifted cocoa, milk, coffee and butter in medium saucepan. Stir over low heat until butter is melted and mixture is smooth (do not allow to boil). Cool.
3 Beat eggs and caster sugar in small bowl with electric mixer until thick and pale. Transfer mixture to large bowl. Stir in sifted flours and chocolate mixture. Pour mixture into prepared tin.

4 Bake about 45 minutes. Stand cake in tin 5 minutes before turning onto wire rack to cool.
5 Serve cake dusted with sifted icing, if desired.

serves 12

dark chocolate mud cake

675g dark eating chocolate,
   chopped
400g unsalted butter, chopped
1½ tablespoons instant coffee
   granules
1¼ cups (310ml) water
1¼ cups (275g) firmly packed
   brown sugar
1¾ cups (260g) plain flour
½ cup (75g) self-raising flour
4 eggs
⅓ cup (80ml) coffee-flavoured
   liqueur
dark chocolate ganache
½ cup (125ml) double cream
400g dark eating chocolate,
   chopped

1 Preheat oven to 160°C/140°C
fan-assisted. Grease deep 19cm-
square cake tin; line with baking
parchment.
2 Combine chocolate, butter,
coffee, the water and sugar in large
saucepan; stir over low heat until
smooth. Cool 15 minutes.
3 Whisk in sifted flours, eggs and
liqueur. Pour mixture into tin; bake
about 2½ hours. Cool cake in tin.
4 Meanwhile, make dark chocolate
ganache.

5 Turn cake, top-side up, onto
plate; spread with ganache. Top
with raspberries, if desired.
dark chocolate ganache Bring
cream to a boil in small saucepan;
remove from heat, add chocolate,
stir until smooth. Refrigerate,
stirring occasionally, about
30 minutes or until spreadable.

serves 16

white chocolate mud cake

180g white chocolate, chopped
350g unsalted butter, chopped
2⅔ cups (590g) caster sugar
1½ cups (375ml) milk
2 cups (300g) plain flour
⅔ cup (100g) self-raising flour
1 teaspoon vanilla extract
3 eggs
white chocolate ganache
½ cup (125ml) double cream
360g white eating chocolate,
   chopped

1 Preheat oven to 160°C/140°C
fan-assisted. Grease deep 22cm-
round cake tin; line with baking
parchment.
2 Combine chocolate, butter, sugar
and milk in large saucepan; stir over
low heat until smooth. Pour mixture
into large bowl; cool 15 minutes.
3 Whisk in sifted flours, extract and
eggs. Pour mixture into tin; bake
about 2 hours. Cool cake in tin.
4 Meanwhile, make white chocolate
ganache.
5 Turn cake, top-side up, onto
plate; spread with ganache.

white chocolate ganache Bring
cream to a boil in small saucepan,
remove from heat; add chocolate,
stir until smooth. Refrigerate,
stirring occasionally, about
30 minutes or until spreadable.

serves 16

150g unsalted butter, chopped
  coarsely
150g dark eating chocolate,
  chopped coarsely
5 eggs, separated
⅔ cup (150g) caster sugar
1½ cups (150g) ground hazelnuts
⅓ cup (45g) roasted hazelnuts,
  chopped coarsely
dark chocolate ganache
⅓ cup (80ml) whipping cream
100g dark eating chocolate,
  chopped coarsely

1 Preheat oven to 160°C/140°C fan-assisted. Grease deep 20cm-round cake tin; line base and sides with baking parchment.
2 Combine butter and chocolate in small saucepan; stir over low heat until smooth. Cool 10 minutes.
3 Beat egg yolks and sugar in medium bowl with electric mixer until thick and pale; beat in chocolate mixture. Beat egg whites in small bowl with electric mixer until soft peaks form. Fold ground hazelnuts into chocolate mixture, then fold in egg white, in two batches. Spoon mixture into tin; bake about 1½ hours.
4 Cool cake in tin. Turn cake, top-side down, onto serving plate.
5 Meanwhile, make dark chocolate ganache.
6 Spread cake with ganache; top with nuts.

dark chocolate ganache Bring cream to the boil in small saucepan. Remove from heat, add chocolate; stir until smooth. Stand 5 minutes before using.

serves 8

rich chocolate hazelnut cake

yogurt fruit loaf

100g butter, softened
2 teaspoons finely grated
  orange rind
¾ cup (165g) caster sugar
2 eggs
2 cups (320g) wholemeal
  self-raising flour
1 cup (280g) plain yogurt
⅓ cup (80ml) orange juice
1 cup (200g) finely chopped
  dried figs
1 cup (150g) coarsely chopped
  raisins

1 Preheat oven to 180°C/160°C
fan-assisted. Grease 14cm x 21cm
loaf tin.
2 Beat butter, rind, sugar, eggs,
flour, yogurt and juice in medium
bowl with electric mixer, on low
speed, until just combined. Stir
in dried fruit.
3 Pour mixture into tin; cover
with foil. Bake 1 hour 15 minutes;
remove foil, bake about a further
15 minutes. Stand loaf 10 minutes;
turn, top-side up, onto wire rack to
cool. Serve at room temperature or
toasted, with butter.

serves 16

pineapple sultana loaf

440g can crushed pineapple in
  juice, drained
1 cup (150g) self-raising flour
½ cup (110g) caster sugar
1 cup (80g) desiccated coconut
1 cup (160g) sultanas
1 egg, beaten lightly
½ cup (125ml) milk

1 Preheat oven to 180°C/160°C
fan-assisted. Grease 14cm x 21cm
loaf tin; line base with baking
parchment, extending paper
5cm above long sides of tin.
2 Combine ingredients in large
bowl. Pour mixture into tin; bake
about 50 minutes. Stand loaf in tin
10 minutes; turn, top-side up, onto
wire rack to cool.

serves 8

boiled fruit cake

2¾ cups (500g) mixed dried fruit
½ cup (125ml) water
1 cup (220g) firmly packed brown
   sugar
125g butter, chopped
1 teaspoon mixed spice
½ teaspoon bicarbonate of soda
½ cup (125ml) sweet sherry
1 egg
1 cup (150g) plain flour
1 cup (150g) self-raising flour
⅓ cup (55g) blanched almonds
2 tablespoons sweet sherry, extra

1 Combine fruit, the water, sugar, butter, spice and soda in large saucepan. Stir over low heat, without boiling, until sugar dissolves and butter melts; bring to a boil. Reduce heat; simmer, covered, 5 minutes. Remove from heat; stir in sherry. Cool to room temperature.
2 Preheat oven to 160°C/140°C fan-assisted. Grease deep 20cm-round cake tin; line base and sides with two layers of baking parchment, extending paper 5cm above side.

3 Stir egg and sifted flours into fruit mixture. Spread mixture into tin; decorate with almonds. Bake about 1½ hours. Brush top of hot cake with extra sherry. Cover cake with foil, cool in tin.

serves 12

egg-free date & nut cake

1 cup (360g) honey
1 cup (250ml) water
30g butter
2¼ cups (360g) wholemeal
   self-raising flour
1 teaspoon mixed spice
½ teaspoon ground ginger
1½ cups (250g) pitted chopped
   dates
¾ cup (90g) chopped walnuts
¼ cup (35g) chopped slivered
   almonds

1 Preheat oven to 180°C/160°C fan-assisted. Grease deep 19cm-square cake tin; line base with baking parchment.
2 Combine honey, water and butter in medium saucepan, stir over low heat until butter melts.
3 Combine sifted flour and spices, dates and nuts in medium bowl; stir in warm honey mixture. Spread cake mixture into prepared tin.
4 Bake about 40 minutes. Stand cake in tin 5 minutes before turning onto wire rack to cool. Glaze with a little extra honey, if desired.

serves 9

glacé fruit cake with ginger syrup

185g butter, softened
½ cup (110g) caster sugar
3 eggs
1 cup (250g) finely chopped
    glacé apricot
½ cup (80g) finely chopped
    glacé orange
½ cup (90g) finely chopped
    glacé ginger
¾ cup (210g) finely chopped
    glacé fig
1½ cups (225g) plain flour
½ cup (75g) self-raising flour
½ cup (125ml) milk
¼ cup (60ml) ginger wine
ginger syrup
¼ cup (60ml) ginger wine
¼ cup (60ml) water
¼ cup (55g) caster sugar
2 teaspoons lemon juice

1 Preheat oven to 150°C/130°C fan-assisted. Line the base and both long sides of 14cm x 21cm loaf tin with baking parchment, extending paper 5cm above sides.
2 Beat butter and sugar in small bowl with electric mixer until just combined. Add eggs, one at a time, beating until just combined between additions; transfer to large bowl. Stir in fruit then sifted flours, and combined milk and wine, in two batches. Spread mixture into tin; bake about 2 hours 30 minutes.
3 Meanwhile, make ginger syrup.
4 Pour hot ginger syrup over hot cake in tin. Cover cake with foil; cool in tin.
ginger syrup Stir ingredients in small saucepan over low heat, without boiling, until sugar dissolves; bring to a boil. Boil, uncovered, without stirring, about 2 minutes or until syrup thickens slightly.

serves 16

last-minute christmas cake

1kg mixed dried fruit
½ cup (100g) glacé cherries, halved
250g butter, chopped
1 cup (200g) firmly packed brown
    sugar
1 cup (250ml) fortified dessert wine
1 cup (150g) coarsely chopped
    brazil nuts
1 tablespoon finely grated orange
    rind
1 tablespoon treacle
5 eggs, beaten lightly
1¾ cups (260g) plain flour
⅓ cup (50g) self-raising flour
½ teaspoon bicarbonate of soda
1 cup (150g) brazil nuts, extra
¼ cup (60ml) fortified dessert wine,
    extra

1 Combine fruit, butter, sugar and wine in large saucepan; stir over low heat until butter is melted and sugar dissolved. Bring to a boil; remove from heat. Transfer to large bowl; cool.

2 Preheat oven to 150°C/130°C fan-assisted. Line base and sides of deep 23cm-square cake tin with two layers brown paper and two layers baking parchment, bringing paper 5cm above sides of tin.

3 Stir nuts, rind, treacle and eggs into fruit mixture, then add sifted dry ingredients. Spread mixture into prepared tin; place extra nuts on top.

4 Bake cake about 2½ hours or until cooked when tested. Brush top of cake with extra wine, cover hot cake tightly with foil; cool in pan.

serves 30

tips This cake can be made three months ahead; store in an airtight container in a cool place or in the refrigerator if the weather is humid. Cake is suitable to freeze for up to three months.

pies, tarts & pastries

Serving up a great looking pie or jewel-coloured fruit tart is always
a pleasure. Making the most of a glut of blackberries or some too-
long-in-the-fruit-bowl apples by baking a pie is to pull triumph from
waste! Mix up your favourite fresh or frozen fruits, experiment with
some warm spices and serve your own creation. If you're not happy
to perfect your pastry making skills, don't worry, with so many options
in the chiller and freezer cabinets, a range of pastries are easy to
buy. Flavour your pie or tart with a syrup, decorate with some pastry
leaves, some sifted sugar or just use your own imagination!

apple pie

10 Granny Smith apples (1.5kg), peeled, cored, sliced thickly
½ cup (125ml) water
¼ cup (55g) caster sugar
1 teaspoon finely grated lemon rind
¼ teaspoon ground cinnamon
1 tablespoon caster sugar, extra
pastry
1 cup (150g) plain flour
½ cup (75g) self-raising flour
¼ cup (35g) cornflour
¼ cup (30g) custard powder
1 tablespoon caster sugar
100g cold butter, chopped
1 egg, separated
¼ cup (60ml) cold water

1 Make pastry.
2 Place apple with the water in large saucepan; bring to a boil. Reduce heat; simmer, covered, about 10 minutes or until apples soften. Drain; stir in sugar, rind and cinnamon. Cool.
3 Preheat oven to 220°C/200°C fan-assisted. Grease deep 25cm pie dish.
4 Divide pastry in half. Roll one half between sheets of baking parchment until large enough to line dish. Spoon apple mixture into dish; brush pastry edge with egg white.

5 Roll remaining pastry large enough to cover filling. Press edges together. Brush pastry with egg white; sprinkle with extra sugar. Bake 20 minutes. Reduce oven temperature to 180°C/160°C fan-assisted; bake a further 25 minutes.
pastry Process dry ingredients and butter until crumbly. Add egg yolk and the water; process until combined. Knead on floured surface until smooth. Cover; refrigerate 30 minutes.

serves 8

apricot & almond apple pie

1 quantity pastry (see apple pie recipe above)
10 medium Granny Smith apples (1.5kg), peeled, cored, sliced thickly
½ cup (125ml) water
1 tablespoon caster sugar
⅔ cup (220g) apricot jam
1 teaspoon finely grated lemon rind
¼ cup (20g) flaked almonds

1 Stew apple with the water, as per step 2 of apple pie recipe. Drain; stir in sugar, jam and rind. Cool.

2 Preheat oven to 220°C/200°C fan-assisted. Grease deep 25cm pie dish.
3 Divide pastry in half. Roll one half between sheets of baking parchment until large enough to line dish. Spoon apple mixture into dish; brush pastry edge with egg white.
4 Roll remaining pastry large enough to cover filling. Press edges together. Brush pastry with egg white; sprinkle with almonds. Bake 20 minutes. Reduce oven temperature to 180°C/160°C fan-assisted; bake a further 25 minutes.

serves 8

9 medium apples (1.5kg)
2 tablespoons caster sugar
1 tablespoon cornflour
1 tablespoon water
300g frozen blackberries
1 tablespoon cornflour, extra
1 tablespoon demerara sugar
pastry
2 cups (300g) plain flour
⅔ cup (110g) icing sugar
185g cold butter, chopped
2 egg yolks
1 tablespoon iced water,
  approximately

1 Peel and core apples; slice thinly. Place in large saucepan with caster sugar; cook, covered, over low heat, about 10 minutes or until apples are just tender. Strain over small saucepan; reserve cooking liquid.
2 Blend cornflour with the water, into reserved cooking liquid over heat until mixture boils and thickens. Place apples in large bowl, gently stir in cornflour mixture; cool to room temperature.
3 Meanwhile, make pastry.
4 Preheat oven to 220°C/200°C fan-assisted.
5 Toss blackberries in extra cornflour; stir gently into apple mixture.
6 Spoon fruit mixture into pastry case; top with rolled pastry. Press edges together, trim with knife; decorate edge. Brush pastry with a little water; sprinkle with demerara sugar. Using knife, make three cuts in top of pastry to allow steam to escape.
7 Place pie on oven tray; bake, uncovered, 20 minutes. Reduce oven temperature to 200°C/180°C fan-assisted; bake, uncovered, about 30 minutes or until pastry is browned lightly. Cool 10 minutes before serving.

pastry Blend or process flour, icing sugar and butter until combined. Add egg yolks and enough of the water to make ingredients just come together. Knead dough on lightly floured surface until smooth. Wrap in cling film, refrigerate 30 minutes. Roll two-thirds of the dough between sheets of baking parchment until large enough to line 23cm-round pie dish. Ease dough into dish; trim edge. Cover; refrigerate 30 minutes. Roll remaining pastry between sheets of baking parchment until large enough to cover pie.

serves 8
tips We used golden delicious apples in this recipe. For a different flavour, replace blackberries with blueberries, raspberries or strawberries. This recipe is best made on the day of serving.

blackberry & apple pie

berry & rhubarb pies

2 cups (220g) coarsely chopped rhubarb
¼ cup (55g) caster sugar
2 tablespoons water
1 tablespoon cornflour
2 cups (300g) frozen mixed berries
1 egg white
2 teaspoons caster sugar, extra
pastry
1⅔ cups (250g) plain flour
⅓ cup (75g) caster sugar
150g cold butter, chopped coarsely
1 egg yolk

1 Make pastry.
2 Place rhubarb, sugar and half the water in medium saucepan; bring to the boil. Reduce heat; simmer, covered, about 3 minutes or until rhubarb is tender. Blend cornflour with the remaining water; stir into rhubarb mixture. Stir over heat until mixture boils and thickens. Remove from heat; stir in berries. Cool.
3 Grease six-hole (180ml) large muffin pan. Roll two-thirds of the pastry between sheets of baking parchment to 4mm thickness; cut out six 12cm rounds. Press rounds into pan holes. Refrigerate 30 minutes.
4 Preheat oven to 200°C/180°C fan-assisted.
5 Roll remaining pastry between sheets of baking parchment to 4mm thickness; cut out six 9cm rounds.
6 Divide fruit mixture among pastry cases.
7 Brush edge of 9cm rounds with egg white; place over filling. Press edges firmly to seal. Brush tops with egg white; sprinkle with extra sugar. Bake about 30 minutes.
8 Stand pies in pan 10 minutes; using palette knife, loosen pies from edge of pan before lifting out. Serve warm with vanilla ice-cream, if desired.

pastry Process flour, sugar and butter until coarse. Add egg yolk; process until combined. Knead on floured surface until smooth. Cover; refrigerate 30 minutes.

makes 6
tips You need four large stems of rhubarb to get the required amount of chopped rhubarb. If pastry is too dry, add 2 teaspoons of water with the egg yolk.

VARIATION
apple & raspberry pies Omit rhubarb and replace with 2 peeled, coarsely chopped medium apples. Cook with sugar and the water for about 5 minutes or until apples are just tender. Omit mixed berries and replace with 150g raspberries.

apple, date & orange pie

8 medium Granny Smith apples
  (1.2kg), peeled, cored, sliced
  thickly
½ cup (125ml) water
1½ cups (210g) coarsely chopped
  dried dates
¼ cup (55g) caster sugar
2 teaspoons finely grated orange
  rind
1 tablespoon demerara sugar
pastry
1 cup (150g) plain flour
½ cup (75g) self-raising flour
¼ cup (35g) cornflour
¼ cup (30g) custard powder
1 tablespoon caster sugar
100g cold butter, chopped
1 egg, separated
¼ cup (60ml) cold water

1 Make pastry.
2 Place apple with the water in
large saucepan; bring to a boil.
Reduce heat; simmer, covered,
about 5 minutes; add dates, cook
a further 5 minutes or until apples
soften. Drain; stir in caster sugar
and rind. Cool.
2 Preheat oven to 220°C/200°C
fan-assisted. Grease deep 25cm
pie dish.
3 Divide pastry in half. Roll one
half between sheets of baking
parchment until large enough to
line dish. Spoon apple mixture
into dish; brush pastry edges with
egg white.
4 Roll remaining pastry large
enough to cover filling. Press edges
together. Brush pastry with egg
white; sprinkle with demerara sugar.
Bake 20 minutes. Reduce oven
temperature to 180°C/160°C fan-
assisted; bake a further 25 minutes.

pastry Process dry ingredients
and butter until crumbly. Add
egg yolk and the water; process
until combined. Knead on floured
surface until smooth. Cover;
refrigerate 30 minutes.

serves 8

1 cup (150g) plain flour
⅓ cup (55g) icing sugar
90g unsalted butter, chopped
1 egg yolk
3 teaspoons iced water,
  approximately
2 tablespoons roasted slivered
  almonds
filling
1 small apple (130g), grated
  coarsely
½ cup (75g) frozen blueberries
1 teaspoon ground cinnamon
2 teaspoons finely grated lemon
  rind

1 Preheat oven to 180°C/160°C fan-assisted. Grease two 12-hole (1-tablespoon/20ml) mini muffin pans.
2 Pulse sifted flour, sugar and butter in food processor until crumbly. Add egg yolk and enough of the water to make mixture come together.
3 Shape one-quarter of the dough into thick sausage; wrap in cling film, freeze 45 minutes.
4 Meanwhile, roll remaining dough to 4mm thickness, cut out 6cm rounds; press dough into holes of pan. Refrigerate 15 minutes.
5 Make filling; divide filling among pastry cases.
6 Coarsely grate frozen dough evenly over filling; sprinkle with nuts. Bake about 20 minutes. Stand 5 minutes; transfer to wire rack to cool.
filling Combine apple, berries, cinnamon and rind in small bowl.

makes 24

blueberry & apple crumble tartlets

apple charlotte tartlets

2 medium green apples (300g),
 peeled, cored
1 tablespoon caster sugar
1 tablespoon water
1 clove
½ teaspoon ground cinnamon
24 x 4.5cm diameter baked pastry
 cases
½ cup (125ml) whipping cream,
 whipped
2 tablespoons passionfruit pulp

1 Thinly slice apples; combine in small saucepan with sugar, the water, clove and cinnamon; cover. Bring to a boil; reduce heat, simmer, covered, about 5 minutes or until apple softens.
2 Drain apple mixture; discard liquid and clove. Cool apple.
3 Place pastry cases on tray, fill with cold stewed apple; refrigerate 30 minutes.
4 Just before serving, top with cream, then drizzle with passionfruit pulp.

makes 24
tip If you would like to make your own pastry cases, see the recipe for pastry in blueberry apple crumble tartlets on page 244.

banoffee pie

395g can sweetened condensed
    milk
75g butter, chopped
½ cup (110g) firmly packed brown
    sugar
2 tablespoons golden syrup
2 large bananas (460g), sliced
    thinly
300ml whipping cream, whipped
pastry
1½ cups (225g) plain flour
1 tablespoon icing sugar
140g cold butter, chopped
1 egg yolk
2 tablespoons cold water

1 Make pastry.
2 Grease 24cm-round loose-based
fluted flan tin. Roll dough between
sheets of baking parchment until
large enough to line tin. Ease
dough into tin; press into base
and side. Trim edge; prick base
all over with fork. Cover; refrigerate
30 minutes.
3 Preheat oven to 200°C/180°C
fan-assisted.
4 Place tin on oven tray; cover
dough with baking parchment,
fill with dried beans or rice. Bake
10 minutes; remove paper and
beans carefully from pie shell.
Bake a further 10 minutes; cool.

5 Meanwhile, combine condensed
milk, butter, sugar and syrup in
medium saucepan; cook over
medium heat, stirring, about
10 minutes or until mixture is
caramel-coloured. Stand 5 minutes;
pour into pie shell, cool.
6 Top caramel with banana; top
with whipped cream.
pastry Process flour, sugar and
butter until crumbly; add egg yolk
and water, process until ingredients
come together. Knead dough on
floured surface until smooth. Wrap
in cling film; refrigerate 30 minutes.

serves 8

banoffee tartlets

395g can sweetened condensed
    milk
2 tablespoons golden syrup
60g unsalted butter
24 x 4.5cm diameter baked
    pastry cases
1 large banana (230g)
½ cup (125ml) whipping cream,
    whipped

1 Combine condensed milk, syrup
and butter in small heavy-based
saucepan; stir over heat until smooth.
2 Bring mixture to a boil; boil,
stirring, about 10 minutes or until
mixture is thick and dark caramel in
colour. Remove pan from heat; cool.
3 Fill pastry cases with caramel; top
with a slice of banana, then a dollop
of cream.

makes 24
tip If you would like to make your
own pastry cases, see the pastry
recipe for in blueberry apple
crumble tartlets on page 244.

apple cream pie

2 medium green apples (300g),
  peeled, sliced thinly
2 eggs
½ cup (110g) caster sugar
2 tablespoons plain flour
2 teaspoons grated lemon rind
1¾ cups (425ml) double cream
250g cream cheese, softened
1 tablespoon mixed peel
¼ cup (40g) raisins, chopped finely
1 teaspoon ground cinnamon
pastry
1¼ cups (185g) plain flour
½ teaspoon ground cinnamon
¼ cup (55g) caster sugar
1 teaspoon baking powder
2 teaspoons grated lemon rind
125g cold butter, chopped coarsely
1 egg yolk
2 tablespoons dry sherry

1 Preheat oven to 2180°C/160°C fan-assisted. Make pastry.
2 Arrange apple in overlapping lines in pastry case. Beat eggs and sugar in small bowl with electric mixer until thick; gradually add flour, beating well between additions. Add rind, ½ cup (125ml) of the cream, cream cheese, peel and raisins; mix well.
3 Pour filling over apples; bake 45 minutes; cool.
4 Beat remaining cream; spread evenly over top of pie. Sprinkle with cinnamon.
pastry Combine flour, cinnamon, sugar, baking powder and rind in medium bowl; rub in butter. Beat egg yolk and sherry in small bowl until combined. Add to flour mixture; mix well. Spread dough evenly over base of 19cm x 29cm rectangular baking tin.

serves 10

1 cup (150g) roasted unsalted
  cashews
1 tablespoon cornflour
¾ cup (165g) firmly packed brown
  sugar
2 tablespoons golden syrup
50g butter, melted
2 eggs
2 tablespoons double cream
1 teaspoon vanilla extract
pastry
1¼ cups (185g) plain flour
¼ cup (55g) caster sugar
125g cold butter, chopped coarsely
1 egg yolk
2 teaspoons water
cinnamon cream
300ml whipping cream
1 tablespoon icing sugar
1 teaspoon ground cinnamon

1 Make pastry.
2 Grease two 12-hole (80ml) muffin pans. Roll pastry between sheets of baking parchment to 3mm thickness; cut out twenty-four 8cm rounds. Press rounds into pan holes; prick bases all over with fork. Refrigerate 20 minutes.
3 Preheat oven to 200°C/180°C fan-assisted.
4 Bake pastry cases 10 minutes. Cool.
5 Reduce temperature to 160°C/140°C fan-assisted.
6 Combine nuts and cornflour in medium bowl; stir in sugar, syrup, butter, egg, cream and extract. Divide filling among pastry cases. Bake about 15 minutes; cool. Refrigerate 30 minutes.
7 Meanwhile, beat ingredients for cinnamon cream in small bowl with electric mixer until soft peaks form. Serve tarts with cinnamon cream.

pastry Process flour, sugar and butter until coarse. Add egg yolk and the water; process until combined. Knead on floured surface until smooth. Cover with cling film; refrigerate 30 minutes.

makes 24
tip If pastry is too dry, add 2 teaspoons of water with the egg yolk.

caramel cashew tarts

mochaccino tartlets

6 frozen unbaked sweet tart
  cases (130g)
80g dark eating chocolate,
  chopped coarsely
2 tablespoons double cream
1 teaspoon instant coffee granules
2 teaspoons coffee-flavoured
  liqueur
2 egg yolks
1 tablespoon caster sugar
2 teaspoons cocoa powder

1 Preheat oven to 180°C/160°C
fan-assisted.
2 Place tart cases on greased and
lined oven tray; bake about
12 minutes. Cool.
3 Combine chocolate, cream,
coffee and liqueur in small
heatproof bowl placed over small
saucepan of simmering water; stir
until smooth. Remove bowl from
pan; cool 5 minutes.
4 Whisk egg yolks and sugar in
small bowl until creamy; fold in
chocolate mixture.

5 Divide filling into cases. Bake for
8 minutes; cool 5 minutes. Chill for
20 minutes before serving.
6 Serve tartlets dusted with sifted
cocoa.
makes 6
tips The tart cases we used were
bought frozen and unbaked;
they come ready-to-bake in foil
cases and measure 6.5cm in
diameter. They are available from
supermarkets. Tartlets can be made
a day ahead, keep refrigerated.

choc-butterscotch tartlets

12 frozen tartlet cases
¼ cup (55g) firmly packed brown
  sugar
20g butter
¼ cup (60ml) double cream
150g dark eating chocolate,
  chopped coarsely
¼ cup (60ml) double cream, extra
2 tablespoons coarsely chopped
  toasted hazelnuts
1 tablespoon cocoa powder

1 Bake tartlet cases according to
manufacturer's instructions.
2 Meanwhile, heat combined sugar,
butter and cream in small saucepan,
stirring until sugar dissolves. Reduce
heat; simmer, uncovered, without
stirring, 2 minutes. Cool 5 minutes.
Stir in chocolate and extra cream;
refrigerate 10 minutes.
3 Divide mixture among tartlet
cases, sprinkle with nuts and sifted
cocoa.

makes 12

crème brûlée praline tarts

1⅓ cups (330ml) double cream
⅓ cup (80ml) milk
1 vanilla pod
4 egg yolks
¼ cup (55g) caster sugar
pastry
1¼ cups (185g) plain flour
¼ cup (55g) caster sugar
125g cold butter, chopped coarsely
1 egg yolk
praline
¼ cup (55g) caster sugar
2 tablespoons water
1 tablespoon roasted hazelnuts
2 tablespoons unsalted roasted
  pistachios

1 Make pastry.
2 Grease six-hole (180ml) large muffin pan. Cut six 11cm rounds from pastry. Press rounds into pan holes; prick bases all over with fork. Refrigerate 30 minutes.
3 Preheat oven to 160°C/140°C fan-assisted.
4 Combine cream and milk in small saucepan. Split vanilla pod in half lengthways; scrape seeds into pan (reserve pod for another use). Bring to the boil. Beat egg yolks and sugar in small bowl with electric mixer until thick and creamy. Gradually whisk hot cream mixture into egg mixture. Pour warm custard into pastry cases.
5 Bake about 30 minutes or until set; cool 15 minutes. Refrigerate 1 hour.
6 Meanwhile, make praline.
7 Preheat grill. Remove tarts from pan; place on oven tray. Sprinkle custard with praline; grill until praline caramelises. Serve immediately.

pastry Process flour, sugar and butter until coarse. Add egg yolk; process until combined. Knead on floured surface until smooth. Roll pastry between sheets of baking parchment to 4mm thickness. Refrigerate 15 minutes.
praline Combine sugar and the water in small saucepan; stir over heat until sugar dissolves. Boil, uncovered, without stirring, about 8 minutes or until golden in colour. Place nuts, in single layer, on greased oven tray. Pour toffee over nuts; stand about 15 minutes or until set. Break toffee into large pieces; process until chopped finely.

makes 6
tip If pastry is too dry, add 2 teaspoons of water with egg yolk.

rich chocolate coconut tart

1 cup (90g) desiccated coconut
1 egg white, beaten lightly
¼ cup (55g) caster sugar
300ml double cream
300g dark eating chocolate,
    chopped finely
4 egg yolks
2 teaspoons coffee-flavoured
    liqueur

1 Preheat oven to 150°C/130°C fan-assisted. Grease 20cm non-stick springform cake tin.
2 Combine coconut, egg white and caster sugar. Press mixture evenly over base and 4cm up sides of prepared tin. Bake, uncovered, about 40 minutes or until golden. Allow to cool.
3 Heat cream until almost boiling. Add chocolate, stir until smooth; cool slightly. Whisk egg yolks and liqueur into chocolate; strain. Pour chocolate mixture into coconut shell. Refrigerate 6 hours or until set.
4 Cut into thin wedges to serve.

serves 12
tips To make it easier to remove tin base from tart, place base in upside down before lining with biscuit. The tart filling is suitable to microwave.

chocolate tartlets

150g dark eating chocolate
¼ cup (60ml) whipping cream
1 tablespoon orange-flavoured
   liqueur
1 egg
2 egg yolks
2 tablespoons caster sugar
pastry
1⅔ cups (250g) plain flour
⅓ cup (75g) caster sugar
150g cold butter, chopped coarsely
1 egg yolk

1 Make pastry.
2 Grease two 12-hole (2-table-spoons/40ml) deep flat-based patty pans.
3 Roll pastry between sheets of baking parchment to 3mm thickness; cut out twenty-four 6.5cm rounds. Press rounds into pan holes; prick bases all over with fork. Refrigerate 30 minutes.
4 Preheat oven to 200°C/180°C fan-assisted.
5 Bake pastry cases 10 minutes. Allow to cool.
6 Reduce oven temperature to 180°C/160°C fan-assisted.
7 Combine chocolate, cream and liqueur in small saucepan; stir over low heat until smooth. Cool 5 minutes.
8 Meanwhile, beat egg, egg yolks and sugar in small bowl with electric mixer until light and fluffy; fold chocolate mixture into egg mixture.
9 Divide filling among pastry cases. Bake 8 minutes; cool 10 minutes. Refrigerate 1 hour. Serve dusted with a little sifted cocoa powder.

pastry Process flour, sugar and butter until coarse. Add egg yolk; process until combined. Knead pastry on floured surface until smooth. Cover with cling film; refrigerate 30 minutes.

makes 24
tip If pastry is too dry, add 2 teaspoons of water with the egg yolk.

½ cup (75g) cornflour
1 cup (220g) caster sugar
½ cup (125ml) lemon juice
1¼ cups (310ml) water
2 teaspoons finely grated lemon
    rind
60g unsalted butter, chopped
3 eggs, separated
½ cup (110g) caster sugar, extra
pastry
1½ cups (225g) plain flour
1 tablespoon icing sugar
140g cold butter, chopped
1 egg yolk
2 tablespoons cold water

1 Make pastry.
2 Grease 24cm-round loose-based fluted flan tin. Roll pastry between sheets of baking parchment until large enough to line tin. Ease pastry into tin, press into base and side; trim edge. Cover; refrigerate 30 minutes.
3 Preheat oven to 240°C/220°C fan-assisted.
4 Place tin on oven tray. Line pastry case with baking parchment; fill with dried beans or rice. Bake 15 minutes; remove paper and beans carefully from pie shell. Bake about 10 minutes; cool pie shell, turn oven off.
5 Meanwhile, combine cornflour and sugar in medium saucepan; gradually stir in juice and the water until smooth. Cook, stirring, over high heat, until mixture boils and thickens. Reduce heat; simmer, stirring, 1 minute. Remove from heat; stir in rind, butter and egg yolks. Cool 10 minutes.

6 Spread filling into pie shell. Cover; refrigerate 2 hours.
7 Preheat oven to 240°C/220°C fan-assisted.
8 Beat egg whites in small bowl with electric mixer until soft peaks form; gradually add extra sugar, beating until sugar dissolves.
9 Roughen surface of filling with fork before spreading with meringue mixture. Bake about 2 minutes or until browned lightly.
pastry Process flour, icing sugar and butter until crumbly. Add egg yolk and the water; process until ingredients come together. Knead dough on floured surface until smooth. Cover; refrigerate 30 minutes.

serves 10

lemon meringue pie

blood orange meringue tarts

½ cup (110g) caster sugar
2 tablespoons cornflour
⅔ cup (160ml) blood orange juice
2 tablespoons water
2 teaspoons finely grated blood
   orange rind
75g unsalted butter, chopped
   coarsely
2 eggs, separated
½ cup (110g) caster sugar, extra
pastry
1¼ cups (185g) plain flour
¼ cup (55g) caster sugar
125g cold butter, chopped coarsely
1 egg yolk

1 Make pastry.
2 Grease 12-hole (80ml) muffin pan. Roll pastry between sheets of baking parchment to 4mm thickness; cut out twelve 8cm rounds. Press rounds into pan holes; prick bases all over with fork. Refrigerate 30 minutes.
3 Preheat oven to 200°C/180°C fan-assisted.
4 Bake pastry cases 10 minutes. Allow to cool.
5 Meanwhile, combine sugar and cornflour in small saucepan; gradually stir in juice and the water until smooth. Cook, stirring, until mixture boils and thickens. Reduce heat; simmer, stirring, 1 minute. Remove from heat; stir in rind, butter and egg yolks. Cool 10 minutes.
6 Divide filling among pastry cases. Refrigerate 1 hour.
7 Increase oven temperature to 240°C/220°C fan-assisted.
8 Beat egg whites in small bowl with electric mixer until soft peaks form; gradually add extra sugar, beating until sugar dissolves.
9 Roughen surface of filling with fork; using star nozzle, pipe meringue over filling. Bake about 3 minutes or until browned lightly.

pastry Process flour, sugar and butter until coarse. Add egg yolk; process until combined. Knead on lightly floured surface until smooth. Cover; refrigerate 30 minutes.

makes 12
tip If pastry is too dry, add 2 teaspoons of water with the egg yolk.

VARIATION
lemon meringue tarts Increase the sugar in filling to ⅔ cup. Omit orange rind and replace with 2 teaspoons finely grated lemon rind. Omit orange juice and replace with ⅔ cup lemon juice.

lemon meringue tartlets

4 egg yolks
⅓ cup (75g) caster sugar
2 teaspoons finely grated lemon
    rind
¼ cup (60ml) lemon juice
40g unsalted butter, chopped
24 x 4.5cm diameter baked pastry
    cases
meringue
1 egg white
¼ cup (55g) caster sugar

1 Combine egg yolks, sugar, rind, juice and butter in small heatproof bowl; stir over small saucepan of simmering water until mixture thickens slightly and coats the back of a spoon. Remove pan from heat, remove bowl from pan immediately; cover surface of lemon curd with cling film; refrigerate until cold.
2 Preheat oven to 200°C/180°C fan-assisted.
3 Meanwhile, make meringue.
4 Place pastry cases on oven tray; fill with curd, then top with meringue.
5 Bake about 5 minutes or until meringue is browned lightly.
meringue Beat egg white in small bowl with electric mixer until soft peaks form; gradually add sugar, beating until dissolved between additions.

makes 24
tip If you would like to make your own delicious pastry cases, see the recipe for pastry in blueberry apple crumble tartlets on page 244.

lime chiffon pie

250g digestive biscuits
125g butter, melted
4 eggs, separated
⅓ cup (75g) caster sugar
3 teaspoons gelatine
2 teaspoons finely grated lime rind
⅓ cup (80ml) lime juice
⅓ cup (80ml) water
⅓ cup (75g) caster sugar, extra

1 Grease deep 23cm pie dish.
2 Process biscuits until fine; add butter, process until combined. Press mixture firmly over base and side of dish; refrigerate 30 minutes.
3 Combine egg yolks, sugar, gelatine, rind, juice and the water in medium heatproof bowl. Whisk over medium saucepan of simmering water until mixture thickens slightly. Remove from heat; pour into large bowl. Cover; cool.
4 Beat egg whites in small bowl with electric mixer until soft peaks form; gradually add extra sugar, beating until sugar dissolves. Fold meringue into filling mixture, in two batches.
5 Spread filling into crumb crust; refrigerate 3 hours.

serves 6
tip This recipe will make eight 8cm pies if the biscuit crumb mixture is doubled; the filling recipe above, however, is sufficient for 8 individual pies.

VARIATION
lemon chiffon pie Replace the finely grated lime rind and juice with finely grated lemon rind and juice.

almond pear flan

1¼ cups (185g) plain flour
90g butter
¼ cup (55g) caster sugar
2 egg yolks
3 firm ripe medium pears (690g),
    peeled, cored, quartered
2 tablespoons apricot jam,
    warmed, strained
almond filling
125g butter
⅓ cup (75g) caster sugar
2 eggs
1 cup (120g) ground almonds
1 tablespoon plain flour

1 Blend or process flour, butter, sugar and egg yolks until just combined. Knead on floured surface until smooth, cover; refrigerate 30 minutes.
2 Meanwhile, make almond filling.
3 Preheat oven to 180°C/160°C fan-assisted. Grease 23cm-round loose-based flan tin.
4 Roll dough between sheets of baking parchment; press dough evenly into base and side of tin. Spread filling into pastry case; arrange pears over filling. Bake about 45 minutes. Brush flan with jam.

almond filling Beat butter and sugar in small bowl with electric mixer until just combined. Add eggs, one at a time; fold in meal and flour.

serves 10
tip Pears can be replaced with apples, peaches, plums, apricots or blueberries.

roasted pear tart

3 medium pears (700g)
1 tablespoon maple syrup
¼ cup (55g) raw sugar
40g butter, chopped
1 sheet ready rolled butter
    puff pastry
1 egg, beaten lightly

1 Preheat oven to 180°C/160°C fan-assisted.
2 Peel pears, leaving stems intact; cut in half lengthways. Remove cores carefully. Place pears in baking dish, cut-side up; top with syrup, sugar and butter.
3 Bake pears about 20 minutes or until tender, brushing pears occasionally with pan juices and turning the pears over after 10 minutes.
4 Increase oven temperature to 200°C/180°C fan-assisted.

5 Cut pastry sheet in half; place pastry halves about 2cm apart on greased oven tray.
6 Place 3 pear halves, cut-side down, on each pastry half. Brush pears and pastry with pan juices, then brush pastry only with a little of the egg.
7 Bake tart about 20 minutes or until pastry is puffed and browned lightly. To serve, cut pastry so each serving contains a pear half.

serves 6

pecan pie

1 cup (120g) pecans, chopped
    coarsely
2 tablespoons cornflour
1 cup (220g) firmly packed brown
    sugar
60g butter, melted
2 tablespoons double cream
1 teaspoon vanilla extract
3 eggs
⅓ cup (40g) pecans, extra
2 tablespoons apricot jam,
    warmed, sieved

pastry
1¼ cups (185g) plain flour
⅓ cup (55g) icing sugar
125g cold butter, chopped
1 egg yolk
1 teaspoon water

1 Make pastry.
2 Grease 24cm-round loose-based flan tin. Roll pastry between sheets of baking parchment until large enough to line tin. Ease pastry into tin, press into base and side; trim edge. Cover; refrigerate 30 minutes.
3 Preheat oven to 180°C/160°C fan-assisted.
4 Place tin on oven tray. Line pastry case with baking parchment, fill with dried beans or rice. Bake 10 minutes; remove paper and beans carefully from pie shell. Bake about 5 minutes; cool.
5 Reduce oven temperature to 160°C/140°C fan-assisted.
6 Combine chopped nuts and cornflour in medium bowl. Add sugar, butter, cream, extract and eggs; stir until combined. Pour mixture into shell, sprinkle with extra nuts.
7 Bake about 45 minutes. Cool; brush pie with jam.

pastry Process flour, icing sugar and butter until crumbly. Add egg yolk and the water; process until ingredients just come together. Knead dough on floured surface until smooth. Cover; refrigerate 30 minutes.

serves 10

mini pecan, macadamia & walnut tarts

1¼ cups (185g) plain flour
⅓ cup (55g) icing sugar
¼ cup (30g) ground almonds
125g cold butter, chopped
1 egg yolk
filling
⅓ cup (50g) macadamias, toasted
⅓ cup (45g) pecans, toasted
⅓ cup (35g) walnuts, toasted
2 tablespoons brown sugar
1 tablespoon plain flour
40g butter, melted
2 eggs, beaten lightly
¾ cup (180ml) maple syrup

1 Grease four 10cm-round loose-based flan tins.
2 Blend or process flour, icing sugar, ground almonds and butter until combined. Add egg yolk; process until ingredients just come together. Knead dough on lightly floured surface until smooth. Wrap in cling film, refrigerate 30 minutes.
3 Divide pastry into quarters. Roll each piece, between sheets of baking parchment, into rounds large enough to line prepared tins; lift pastry into each tin. Press into sides; trim edges. Cover; refrigerate 30 minutes.
4 Meanwhile, preheat oven to 200°C/180°C fan-assisted.
5 Place tins on oven tray. Line each tin with baking parchment, fill with dried beans or rice. Bake, uncovered, 10 minutes. Remove paper and beans. Bake, uncovered, a further 7 minutes or until pastry cases are browned lightly.

6 Reduce oven temperature to 180°C/160°C fan-assisted.
7 Divide filling among cases. Bake about 25 minutes or until set; cool.
filling Combine ingredients in medium bowl; mix well.

serves 4
tips Do not use maple-flavoured syrup as a substitute for the 'real thing' in the nut filling. To toast nuts, place in a heavy-based frying pan, stir nuts constantly over medium-to-high heat, until they are evenly browned. Remove from pan immediately.

lemon tart

1¼ cups (185g) plain flour
¼ cup (40g) icing sugar
¼ cup (30g) ground almonds
125g cold butter, chopped
1 egg yolk
lemon filling
1 tablespoon finely grated lemon
   rind
½ cup (125ml) lemon juice
5 eggs
¾ cup (165g) caster sugar
1 cup (250ml) whipping cream

1 Blend or process flour, icing sugar, ground almonds and butter until combined. Add egg yolk, process until ingredients just come together. Knead dough on lightly floured surface until smooth. Wrap in cling film, refrigerate 30 minutes.
2 Roll pastry between sheets of baking parchment until large enough to line 24cm-round loose-based flan tin. Ease dough into tin; trim edge. Cover; refrigerate 30 minutes.
3 Meanwhile, preheat oven to 200°C/180°C fan-assisted.
4 Place tin on oven tray. Line pastry case with baking parchment, fill with dried beans or rice. Bake, uncovered, 15 minutes. Remove paper and beans; bake, uncovered, a further 10 minutes or until browned lightly.

5 Meanwhile, make lemon filling.
6 Reduce oven to 180°C/160°C fan-assisted.
7 Pour lemon filling into pastry case, bake about 30 minutes or until filling has set slightly; cool.
8 Refrigerate until cold. Serve dusted with sifted icing sugar, if desired.
lemon filling Whisk ingredients in medium bowl; stand 5 minutes.

serves 8
tip This tart tastes even better if made the day before required; keep, covered in refrigerator. You need about three medium lemons (420g) for this tart.

½ cup (110g) caster sugar
2 tablespoons cornflour
3 egg yolks
¾ cup (180ml) milk
½ cup (125ml) double cream
1 vanilla pod, split lengthways
5cm strip lemon rind
1 sheet ready-rolled butter puff
   pastry

1 Preheat oven to 220°C/200°C fan-assisted. Grease two 12-hole (1-tablespoon/20ml) mini muffin pans.
2 Combine sugar and cornflour in medium saucepan. Gradually whisk in combined egg yolks, milk and cream.
3 Scrape vanilla seeds into custard; add rind. Stir over medium heat until mixture just comes to the boil. Remove from heat; discard rind. Cover surface of custard with cling film while making pastry cases.

4 Cut pastry sheet in half; place two halves on top of each other. Roll pastry up tightly from long side; cut log into 24 rounds.
5 Roll each pastry round on floured surface to 6cm diameter. Press pastry into pan holes.
6 Divide custard among pastry cases. Bake about 12 minutes. Turn, top-side up, onto wire rack to cool. Serve dusted with a little sifted icing sugar.

makes 24

portuguese custard tartlets

baklava fig tarts

6 sheets filo pastry
50g butter, melted
12 large fresh figs (960g)
⅓ cup (75g) firmly packed brown
   sugar
1 teaspoon mixed spice
½ teaspoon ground cinnamon
80g butter, chopped coarsely
½ cup (60g) finely chopped roasted
   walnuts
¼ cup (35g) slivered almonds
1 teaspoon finely grated orange
   rind
maple cream
300ml whipping cream
2 tablespoons maple syrup

1 Preheat oven to 200°C/180°C fan-assisted. Grease 12-hole (80ml) muffin pan.
2 Brush three pastry sheets with melted butter; stack together. Repeat with remaining pastry. Cut each pastry stack into six rectangles (you will have 12 rectangles). Gently press one stack into each pan hole.
3 Quarter each fig, cutting three-quarters of the way down the fig. Place one fig in each pastry case.
4 Combine sugar and spices in medium bowl; using fingers, rub in chopped butter. Stir in nuts and rind; gently push mixture into the centre of figs. Bake about 15 minutes.
5 Meanwhile, make maple cream.
6 Serve baklava fig tarts dusted with a little sifted icing sugar, and maple cream.
maple cream Beat cream and syrup in small bowl with electric mixer until soft peaks form.

makes 12

pies, tarts & pastries

apple tarte tartin

6 medium golden delicious
   apples (900g)
2 tablespoons lemon juice
4 sheets ready-rolled butter
   puff pastry
1 cup (220g) caster sugar
100g unsalted butter, chopped
   coarsely
¼ cup (60ml) water

1 Preheat oven to 200°C/180°C fan-assisted.
2 Peel, core and quarter apples; combine apples and juice in medium bowl.
3 Brush two pastry sheets with water; top with remaining sheets, press sheets firmly together. Cut an 18cm round from both pastry sheets.
4 Combine sugar, butter and the water in medium frying pan; stir over heat until sugar dissolves. Bring to the boil; reduce heat, simmer, without stirring, about 15 minutes, shaking pan occasionally, until dark caramel in colour. Allow bubbles to subside, carefully pour caramel into two shallow 16cm-round fluted metal pie tins. Add ¼ cup water to the hot frying pan; reserve caramel.

5 Position apple quarters in tins. Cut any remaining apples in half and place in tins to fill in any gaps.
6 Brush apples with reserved caramel; cover tarts with foil, bake 15 minutes.
7 Remove foil from tarts; carefully top apples with pastry rounds, tuck pastry down between the side of the tin and the apples. Bake about 30 minutes or until pastry is golden brown.
8 Stand 1 hour before turning onto serving plate.

serves 8

berry sponge pie

2 sheets ready-rolled sweet
  puff pastry, thawed
3 eggs
½ cup (110g) caster sugar
½ cup (75g) self-raising flour
1½ cups (225g) frozen mixed
  berries
1 egg white, beaten lightly
1 tablespoon caster sugar, extra
1 tablespoon icing sugar

1 Preheat oven to 220°C/200°C fan-assisted. Grease 25cm x 30cm swiss roll tin.
2 Roll one pastry sheet until large enough to cover base of pan, extending pastry halfway up sides. Prick pastry with fork at 2cm intervals; freeze 5 minutes.
3 Place another swiss roll tin on top of pastry; bake 5 minutes. Remove top tin; bake further 5 minutes or until pastry is browned lightly. Cool 5 minutes.

4 Meanwhile, beat eggs and sugar in small bowl with electric mixer until thick and creamy; fold in sifted flour. Spread mixture evenly over pastry; sprinkle evenly with berries.
5 Roll remaining pastry sheet large enough to fit tin; place over berries. Brush pastry with egg white, sprinkle with extra sugar; score pastry in crosshatch pattern.
6 Bake about 20 minutes. Cool in tin; dust with sifted icing sugar then cut into squares.

serves 20

berry custard pastries

2 sheets ready-rolled butter puff
  pastry, thawed
1 tablespoon icing sugar
700g mixed fresh berries
1 tablespoon icing sugar, extra
custard cream
300ml whipping cream
300g thick vanilla custard
¼ cup (40g) icing sugar

1 Preheat oven to 220°C/200°C fan-assisted. Grease three oven trays; line with baking parchment.
2 Make custard cream; cover, refrigerate 30 minutes or until firm.
3 Meanwhile, cut one pastry sheet in half. Sprinkle one half with half of the sugar; place other pastry half on top. Roll pastry up tightly from short side; cut log into eight rounds. Repeat with remaining pastry sheet and remaining sugar.
4 Place pastry rounds, cut-side up, on board dusted lightly with icing sugar; roll each round into an oval about 8cm x 10cm. Place on trays.

5 Bake pastries about 12 minutes.
6 Place a drop of the custard cream on each of eight serving plates; top each with a pastry. Divide half of the berries over pastries, then top with custard cream, remaining berries and remaining pastries. Dust with extra sifted icing sugar.
custard cream Beat cream, custard and sifted icing sugar in small bowl with electric mixer until soft peaks form.

serves 8

apple & prune pastry slice

4 medium apples (600g)
¾ cup (135g) coarsely chopped
    pitted prunes
2½ cups (625ml) water
½ teaspoon ground cinnamon
½ teaspoon ground nutmeg
2 tablespoons ground hazelnuts
2 sheets ready-rolled shortcrust
    pastry, thawed
1 tablespoon caster sugar

1 Peel and core apples; slice thinly. Place apples and prunes in medium saucepan with the water, bring to a boil. Reduce heat, simmer, covered, 10 minutes or until apples are just tender. Drain well; cool 15 minutes.
2 Combine cinnamon, nutmeg and ground hazelnuts in medium bowl; gently stir in apple mixture.
3 Preheat oven to 200°C/180°C fan-assisted. Grease 20cm x 30cm baking tin; line base with baking parchment.
4 Roll one pastry sheet large enough to cover base of tin; place in tin, trim edges. Cover pastry with baking parchment, fill with dried beans or rice; bake 15 minutes. Remove paper and beans; bake 5 minutes. Spread apple mixture over pastry.
5 Roll remaining pastry sheet large enough to fit tin; place over apple filling. Brush pastry with a little water, sprinkle with sugar; score pastry in crosshatch pattern. Bake about 45 minutes. Cool in tin; cut into squares.

makes 24

puddings & desserts

For most of us today, desserts are treats to be relished when we're eating out, have guests or are having a special family meal, rather than something we eat every day. All the more applause for the cook, then, when something sweet and beautiful appears to crown the meal. Here we offer some beloved classics, all-time favourites and decadent temptations; some are simple and quick to put together, others are more time-consuming, but worth it.

soft-centred mocha puddings

150g dark eating chocolate,
  chopped coarsely
125g butter, chopped coarsely
3 teaspoons instant coffee
  granules
2 eggs
2 egg yolks
⅓ cup (75g) caster sugar
¼ cup (35g) plain flour
2 teaspoons cocoa powder

1 Preheat oven to 200°C/180°C fan-assisted. Grease six-hole (180ml) large muffin pan well with softened butter.
2 Stir chocolate, butter and coffee in small saucepan, over low heat, until smooth; cool 10 minutes. Transfer to a large bowl.
3 Beat eggs, egg yolks and sugar in small bowl with electric mixer until thick and creamy. Fold egg mixture and sifted flour into barely warm chocolate mixture.
4 Divide mixture among pan holes; bake puddings 12 minutes.
5 Gently turn onto serving plates, top-side down. Serve puddings immediately, dusted with sifted cocoa powder. Serve with whipped cream and fresh raspberries.

makes 6
tip Use a good-quality dark chocolate with 70% cocoa solids.

summer pudding

3 eggs
½ cup (110g) caster sugar
1 tablespoon cornflour
¾ cup (110g) self-raising flour
1 teaspoon butter
¼ cup (60ml) boiling water
⅓ cup (75g) caster sugar, extra
½ cup (125ml) water
2 cups (300g) frozen blackberries
3⅓ cups (500g) frozen mixed
  berries
¼ cup (80g) blackberry jam

1 Preheat oven to 180°C/160°C fan-assisted. Grease 25cm x 30cm swiss roll tin; line base with baking parchment, extending paper 5cm over long sides.
2 Beat eggs in small bowl with electric mixer until thick and creamy. Gradually add sugar, beating until sugar dissolves; transfer mixture to large bowl.
3 Fold triple-sifted flours into egg mixture. Pour combined butter and boiling water down side of bowl; fold into egg mixture. Spread mixture into tin; bake 15 minutes. Cool in tin.
4 Meanwhile, combine extra sugar and the water in medium saucepan; bring to a boil. Stir in berries; return to a boil. Reduce heat; simmer, uncovered, until berries soften. Strain over medium bowl; reserve syrup and berries separately.
5 Turn cake onto board. Line 1.25-litre pudding basin with cling film, extending film 10cm over side of basin. Cut circle slightly smaller than top edge of basin from cake using tip of sharp knife; cut second circle exact size of base of basin from cake. Cut remaining cake into 10cm long strips.

6 Place small cake circle in base of basin and use cake strips to line side of basin. Pour ⅔ cup of the reserved syrup into small jug; reserve. Fill basin with berries; cover with remaining syrup, top with large cake circle. Cover pudding with overhanging cling film, weight pudding with saucer; refrigerate 3 hours or overnight.
7 Stir jam and two tablespoons of the reserved syrup in small saucepan until heated through. Turn pudding onto serving plate; brush with remaining reserved syrup then jam mixture. Serve with whipped cream, if desired.

serves 6

bread & butter pudding

6 slices white bread (270g)
40g butter, softened
½ cup (80g) sultanas
¼ teaspoon ground nutmeg
custard
1½ cups (375ml) milk
2 cups (500ml) double cream
⅓ cup (75g) caster sugar
½ teaspoon vanilla extract
4 eggs

1 Preheat oven to 160°C/140°C fan-assisted.
2 Make custard.
3 Grease shallow 2-litre ovenproof dish. Trim crusts from bread. Spread each slice with butter; cut into 4 triangles. Layer bread, overlapping, in dish; sprinkle with sultanas. Pour custard over bread; sprinkle with nutmeg.

4 Place dish in large baking dish; add enough boiling water to come halfway up sides of dish. Bake about 45 minutes or until pudding sets. Remove pudding from baking dish; stand 5 minutes before serving.
custard Combine milk, cream, sugar and extract in medium saucepan; bring to a boil. Whisk eggs in large bowl; whisking constantly, gradually add hot milk mixture to egg mixture.

serves 6

chocolate pecan pudding

1 quantity custard (see bread and butter pudding recipe, above)
200g ciabatta, sliced thickly
100g dark eating chocolate, chopped coarsely
⅓ cup (40g) coarsely chopped roasted pecans

1 Preheat oven to 160°C/140°C fan-assisted.
2 Grease shallow 2-litre ovenproof dish. Layer bread, chocolate and nuts, overlapping slices slightly, in dish. Pour custard over bread.
3 Place dish in large baking dish; add enough boiling water to come halfway up sides of dish. Bake about 45 minutes or until pudding sets. Remove pudding from baking dish; stand 5 minutes before serving.

serves 6

mincemeat & brioche pudding

475g jar mincemeat
2 tablespoons brandy
300g brioche, sliced thickly
1 tablespoon demerara sugar
custard
1½ cups (375ml) milk
2 cups (500ml) double cream
⅓ cup (75g) caster sugar
½ teaspoon vanilla extract
4 eggs

1 Preheat oven to 160°C/140°C fan-assisted.
2 Make custard.
3 Combine mincemeat and brandy in small bowl.
4 Grease shallow 2-litre ovenproof dish. Layer bread and half the fruit mixture, overlapping bread slightly, in dish. Dollop spoonfuls of remaining fruit mixture over bread. Pour custard over bread; sprinkle with sugar.

5 Place dish in large baking dish; add enough boiling water to come halfway up sides of dish. Bake about 45 minutes or until pudding sets. Remove pudding from baking dish; stand 5 minutes before serving.
custard Combine milk, cream, sugar and extract in medium saucepan; bring to a boil. Whisk eggs in large bowl; whisking constantly, gradually add hot milk mixture to egg mixture.

serves 6

impossible pudding

½ cup (75g) plain flour
1 cup (220g) caster sugar
¾ cup (60g) desiccated coconut
4 eggs
1 teaspoon vanilla extract
125g butter, melted
½ cup (40g) flaked almonds
2 cups (500ml) milk

You'll discover when you make this pudding how it got its name: when cooked, the pudding magically separates into three perfect layers. Impossible!

1 Preheat oven to 180°C/160°C fan-assisted. Grease deep 24cm pie dish.
2 Combine sifted flour, sugar, coconut, eggs, extract, butter and half the nuts in large bowl; gradually add milk, stirring, until combined. Pour into dish; bake 35 minutes.
3 Remove from oven. Sprinkle remaining nuts over pudding; bake 10 minutes. Serve pudding with cream or fruit, if desired.

serves 8

white chocolate & raspberry bread puddings

3 small croissants (150g)
100g white eating chocolate,
    chopped coarsely
1 cup (150g) fresh raspberries
1¼ cups (310ml) milk
¾ cup (180ml) double cream
2 tablespoons caster sugar
½ teaspoon vanilla extract
3 eggs

1 Preheat oven to 160°C/140°C fan-assisted. Grease six-hole (180ml) large muffin pan; line each pan hole with two criss-crossed 5cm x 20cm strips of baking parchment.
2 Split each croissant in half lengthways then tear each half into pieces. Roughly line each pan hole with croissant pieces. Sprinkle with chocolate and berries.
3 Combine milk, cream, sugar and extract in small saucepan; bring to the boil. Whisk eggs in large bowl; gradually whisk in hot milk mixture. Pour custard into pan holes.
4 Place pan in large baking dish; add enough boiling water to come halfway up sides of pan. Bake about 35 minutes or until puddings set. Remove pan from dish; stand puddings 15 minutes. Using baking parchment strips, lift puddings from pan holes onto serving plates. Serve dusted with a little sifted icing sugar. Serve accompanied by fresh raspberries.

makes 6

VARIATION
dark chocolate & fig bread pudding Omit the white chocolate and replace with 100g coarsely chopped dark eating chocolate. Omit the raspberries and replace with 2 coarsely chopped fresh large figs.

golden syrup dumplings

1¼ cups (185g) self-raising flour
30g butter
⅓ cup (115g) golden syrup
⅓ cup (80ml) milk
syrup sauce
30g butter
¾ cup (165g) firmly packed brown
   sugar
½ cup (175g) golden syrup
1⅔ cups (410ml) water

1 Sift flour into medium bowl; rub in butter. Gradually stir in golden syrup and milk.
2 Make syrup sauce.
3 Drop rounded tablespoonfuls of mixture into simmering sauce; simmer, covered, about 20 minutes. Serve dumplings with sauce.
syrup sauce Combine ingredients in medium saucepan; stir over heat, without boiling, until sugar dissolves. Bring to a boil, without stirring. Reduce heat; simmer, uncovered, 5 minutes.

serves 4

coffee & pecan puddings

¾ cup (90g) coarsely chopped
   toasted pecans
300ml double cream
1½ cups (330g) firmly packed
   brown sugar
100g cold butter, chopped
125g butter, softened
1 teaspoon vanilla extract
½ cup (110g) caster sugar
2 eggs
1 cup (150g) self-raising flour
¼ cup (35g) plain flour
¼ cup (60ml) milk
1 tablespoon finely ground
   espresso coffee

1 Preheat oven to 180°C/160°C fan-assisted. Grease six ¾-cup (180ml) metal moulds or ovenproof dishes; line bases with baking parchment.
2 Divide nuts among moulds; place moulds on oven tray.
3 Stir cream, brown sugar and chopped butter in small saucepan over heat, without boiling, until sugar dissolves. Reduce heat; simmer, uncovered, without stirring, about 5 minutes or until mixture thickens slightly. Spoon 2 tablespoons of the sauce over nuts in each mould; reserve remaining sauce.

4 Beat softened butter, extract and caster sugar in small bowl with electric mixer until light and fluffy. Add eggs, one at a time, beating until just combined between additions. Stir in sifted flours, milk and coffee; divide mixture among moulds. Bake puddings, uncovered, 30 minutes. Stand 5 minutes before turning onto serving plates.
5 Reheat reserved sauce. Serve puddings with sauce.

serves 6

sticky banana puddings with butterscotch sauce

125g butter, softened
⅔ cup (150g) firmly packed brown
   sugar
2 eggs
1½ cups (225g) self-raising flour
1 teaspoon mixed spice
1 cup (230g) mashed banana
¼ cup (60g) soured cream
¼ cup (60ml) milk
2 tablespoons brown sugar, extra
1 large banana (230g), sliced thinly
butterscotch sauce
½ cup (110g) firmly packed brown
   sugar
⅔ cup (160ml) double cream
50g butter

1 Preheat oven to 180°C/160°C fan-assisted. Grease eight holes of two six-hole (180ml) large muffin pans.
2 Beat butter and sugar in small bowl with electric mixer until light and fluffy. Beat in eggs, one at a time; transfer mixture to large bowl. Stir in sifted flour and spice, mashed banana, soured cream and milk in two batches.
3 Sprinkle extra sugar in pan holes; cover bases of pan holes with sliced banana. Divide cake mixture among pan holes. Bake 30 minutes.
4 Meanwhile, make butterscotch sauce.
5 Turn puddings, top-side down, onto serving plates; serve warm with butterscotch sauce and vanilla ice-cream.

butterscotch sauce Combine ingredients in small saucepan; stir over heat, without boiling, until sugar dissolves. Simmer, stirring, about 3 minutes or until sauce thickens slightly.

makes 8
tip You need 2 large (460g) over-ripe bananas to get the required amount of mashed banana for this recipe.

chocolate self-saucing pudding

60g butter
½ cup (125ml) milk
½ teaspoon vanilla extract
¾ cup (165g) caster sugar
1 cup (150g) self-raising flour
1 tablespoon cocoa powder
¾ cup (165g) firmly packed brown
  sugar
1 tablespoon cocoa powder, extra
2 cups (500ml) boiling water

1 Preheat oven to 180°C/160°C
fan-assisted. Grease 1.5-litre ovenproof dish.
2 Melt butter with milk in medium
saucepan. Remove from heat; stir in
extract and caster sugar then sifted
flour and cocoa. Spread mixture
into dish.

3 Sift brown sugar and extra cocoa
over mixture; gently pour boiling
water over mixture. Bake about
40 minutes or until centre is firm.
Stand 5 minutes before serving.

serves 6

date & butterscotch self-saucing pudding

1 cup (150g) self-raising flour
½ cup (110g) firmly packed brown
  sugar
20g butter, melted
½ cup (125ml) milk
½ cup (70g) finely chopped dried
  pitted dates
caramel sauce
½ cup (110g) firmly packed brown
  sugar
1¾ cups (430ml) boiling water
50g butter

1 Preheat oven to 180°C/160°C
fan-assisted. Grease 2-litre shallow
ovenproof dish.
2 Combine flour, sugar, butter, milk
and dates in medium bowl. Spread
mixture into dish.
3 Make caramel sauce.
4 Pour caramel sauce slowly over
back of spoon onto mixture in
dish. Bake about 45 minutes or
until centre is firm. Stand 5 minutes
before serving.
caramel sauce Combine
ingredients in medium heatproof
jug; stir until sugar is dissolved.

serves 6

mocha, pear & hazelnut self-saucing pudding

100g dark eating chocolate, chopped
150g butter
⅔ cup (160ml) milk
1½ tablespoons instant coffee granules
⅔ cup (70g) ground hazelnuts
¾ cup (165g) firmly packed brown sugar
1 cup (150g) self-raising flour
1 egg
2 medium pears (460g), sliced thinly
1¾ cups (430ml) water
¾ cup (165g) firmly packed brown sugar, extra
½ cup (50g) cocoa powder

1 Preheat oven to 180°C/160°C fan-assisted. Grease eight 310ml individual ovenproof dishes or a shallow 2.5-litre ovenproof dish.
2 Stir chocolate, 50g of the butter, milk and coffee in small saucepan over low heat until smooth. Transfer to large bowl; stir in ground hazelnuts, sugar, then sifted flour and egg.
3 Place pear slices, slightly overlapping, in dishes; top with chocolate mixture.
4 Stir the water, extra sugar, sifted cocoa and remaining butter in small saucepan over low heat until smooth; pour over chocolate mixture. Bake about 30 minutes (or about 45 minutes for larger pudding). Stand 5 minutes before serving.

serves 8

college pudding

⅓ cup (110g) raspberry jam
1 egg
½ cup (110g) caster sugar
1 cup (150g) self-raising flour
½ cup (125ml) milk
25g butter, melted
1 tablespoon boiling water
1 teaspoon vanilla extract

1 Grease four 250ml metal moulds; divide jam among moulds.
2 Beat egg and sugar in small bowl with electric mixer until thick and creamy. Fold in sifted flour and milk, in two batches; fold in combined butter, the water and extract.
3 Top jam with pudding mixture. Cover each mould with pleated baking parchment and foil (to allow puddings to expand as they cook); secure with kitchen string.
4 Place puddings in large pan with enough boiling water to come halfway up sides of moulds. Cover pan with tight-fitting lid; boil 25 minutes, replenishing water as necessary to maintain level. Stand puddings 5 minutes before turning onto plate. Serve with cream, if desired.

serves 4

VARIATION
golden syrup Replace the jam with ⅓ cup golden syrup.

lemon delicious pudding

125g butter, melted
2 teaspoons finely grated lemon
 rind
1½ cups (330g) caster sugar
3 eggs, separated
½ cup (75g) self-raising flour
⅓ cup (80ml) lemon juice
1⅓ cups (330ml) milk

1 Preheat oven to 180°C/160°C fan-assisted. Grease six 250ml individual ovenproof dishes.
2 Combine butter, rind, sugar and yolks in large bowl. Stir in sifted flour then juice. Gradually stir in milk; mixture should be smooth and runny.
3 Beat egg whites in small bowl with electric mixer until soft peaks form; fold into lemon mixture, in two batches.

4 Place ovenproof dishes in large baking dish; divide lemon mixture among dishes. Add enough boiling water to baking dish to come halfway up sides of ovenproof dishes. Bake, uncovered, about 45 minutes.

serves 6

lemon meringue pudding

200g bought sponge cake
1¾ cups (430ml) double cream
1 teaspoon vanilla extract
1 teaspoon finely grated lemon
 rind
⅓ cup (80ml) lemon juice
6 eggs
¾ cup (165g) caster sugar
280g jar lemon butter
1 tablespoon caster sugar, extra
yellow food colouring
meringue
3 egg whites
¾ cup (165g) caster sugar

1 Preheat oven to 170°C/150°C fan-assisted. Lightly grease round 2-litre ovenproof dish.
2 Cut sponge cake into 3cm pieces; place pieces randomly in dish. Combine cream, extract, rind and juice in small saucepan over low heat, stirring until hot.
3 Whisk eggs and sugar in large bowl until combined. Whisking constantly, pour hot cream mixture into egg mixture; pour into dish over sponge cake. Bake, uncovered, 45 minutes. Remove pudding from oven; increase oven temperature to 180°C/160°C fan-assisted.
4 Cool pudding for 10 minutes.

5 Using a rubber spatula, carefully spread lemon butter over surface.
6 Make meringue. Spoon meringue over pudding to completely cover surface. Tint extra sugar with a little yellow colouring in small bowl; sprinkle yellow sugar evenly over meringue. Bake, uncovered, about 15 minutes or until browned lightly. Serve hot with cream or ice-cream, if desired.
meringue Beat egg whites in small bowl with electric mixer until soft peaks form; add sugar, a tablespoon at a time, beating until sugar dissolves between additions.

serves 8

60g butter
¼ cup (90g) golden syrup
½ teaspoon bicarbonate of soda
1 cup (150g) self-raising flour
2 teaspoons ground ginger
½ cup (125ml) milk
1 egg
syrup
⅓ cup (115g) golden syrup
2 tablespoons water
30g butter

1 Grease 1.25-litre pudding basin.
2 Combine butter and syrup in small saucepan; stir over low heat until smooth. Remove from heat, stir in bicarbonate of soda; transfer mixture to medium bowl. Stir in sifted dry ingredients then combined milk and egg, in two batches.
3 Spread mixture into basin. Cover with pleated baking parchment and foil; secure with lid.
4 Place pudding steamer in large saucepan with enough boiling water to come halfway up side of basin; cover pan with tight-fitting lid. Boil 1 hour, replenishing water as necessary to maintain level. Stand pudding 5 minutes before turning onto plate.

5 Meanwhile, make syrup.
6 Serve pudding topped with syrup and, if desired, pouring cream.
syrup Stir ingredients in small saucepan over heat until smooth; bring to a boil. Reduce heat; simmer, uncovered, 2 minutes.

serves 6

steamed ginger pudding

queen of puddings

2 cups (140g) stale breadcrumbs
1 tablespoon caster sugar
1 teaspoon vanilla extract
1 teaspoon finely grated lemon
  rind
2½ cups (625ml) milk
60g butter
4 eggs, separated
¼ cup (80g) raspberry jam, warmed
¾ cup (165g) caster sugar, extra

1 Preheat oven to 180°C/160°C fan-assisted. Grease six ¾-cup (180ml) individual ovenproof dishes; stand on oven tray.
2 Combine breadcrumbs, sugar, extract and rind in large bowl. Heat milk and butter in medium saucepan until almost boiling, pour over breadcrumb mixture; stand 10 minutes. Stir in yolks.
3 Divide mixture among dishes. Bake about 30 minutes. Carefully spread jam over top of hot puddings.
4 Beat egg whites in small bowl with electric mixer until soft peaks form; gradually add extra sugar, beating until sugar dissolves. Spoon meringue over puddings; bake about 10 minutes.

serves 6

2 medium apples (300g)
80g butter
¾ cup (165g) firmly packed
  brown sugar
125g butter, softened, extra
⅔ cup (150g) caster sugar
1 teaspoon vanilla extract
2 eggs
1 cup (150g) self-raising flour
⅔ cup (100g) plain flour
½ teaspoon bicarbonate of soda
1 cup (250ml) buttermilk
¾ cup (180ml) double cream

1 Preheat oven to 180°C/160°C fan-assisted. Grease 20cm bundt tin.
2 Peel, core and quarter apples; slice thinly. Melt butter in large frying pan; cook apple about 5 minutes or until browned lightly. Add brown sugar; cook, stirring, about 5 minutes or until mixture thickens slightly. Strain apples over medium bowl. Reserve apples and cooking liquid.
3 Beat extra butter, caster sugar and extract in small bowl with electric mixer until light and fluffy. Add eggs, one at a time, beating until just combined between additions; transfer to large bowl. Stir in sifted dry ingredients and buttermilk, in two batches.

4 Spread two-thirds of the mixture into tin. Top with apples, leaving a 2cm border around the edge; cover with remaining mixture. Bake about 50 minutes. Stand cake 5 minutes; turn, top-side up, onto wire rack to cool.
5 Meanwhile, return reserved apple liquid to large frying pan, add cream; bring to a boil. Reduce heat; simmer, uncovered, about 15 minutes or until sauce thickens.
6 Serve warm pudding with caramel sauce.

serves 8

caramelised apple butter pudding

sticky toffee, date & banana pudding

1½ cups (330g) caster sugar
1½ cups (375ml) water
3 star anise
2 medium bananas (400g), sliced
  thinly
1 cup (140g) dried pitted dates
¾ cup (180ml) water, extra
½ cup (125ml) dark rum
1 teaspoon bicarbonate of soda
60g butter, chopped
½ cup (110g) firmly packed
  brown sugar
2 eggs
2 teaspoons mixed spice
1 cup (150g) self-raising flour
½ cup (115g) mashed banana
300ml whipping cream

1 Preheat oven to 180°C/160°C fan-assisted. Grease deep 22cm-round cake tin; line base with baking parchment.
2 Stir caster sugar, the water and star anise in medium saucepan over low heat, without boiling, until sugar dissolves. Bring to a boil; boil syrup, uncovered, without stirring, about 5 minutes or until thickened slightly. Strain ½ cup of the syrup into small heatproof jug; reserve to flavour cream. Discard star-anise.
3 To make toffee, continue boiling remaining syrup, uncovered, without stirring, about 10 minutes or until toffee is golden brown. Pour hot toffee into cake tin; top with sliced banana.

4 Combine dates, the extra water and rum in small saucepan; bring to a boil then remove from heat. Stir in soda; stand 5 minutes. Blend or process date mixture with butter and brown sugar until almost smooth. Add eggs, spice and flour; blend or process until just combined. Stir in mashed banana.
5 Pour mixture into tin; bake about 40 minutes. Turn cake, in tin, onto serving plate; stand 2 minutes. Remove tin then baking parchment.
6 To make star anise cream, beat cream in small bowl with electric mixer until firm peaks form. Stir in reserved syrup.
7 Serve cake warm or at room temperature with star anise cream.

serves 8

1½ cups (250g) pitted dried dates
1¼ cups (310ml) boiling water
1 teaspoon bicarbonate of soda
¾ cup (165g) firmly packed brown
   sugar
60g butter, chopped
2 eggs
1 cup (150g) self-raising flour
caramel sauce
1 cup (220g) firmly packed brown
   sugar
100g butter, chopped
300ml double cream

1 Preheat oven to 180°C/160°C fan-assisted. Grease 22cm-round cake tin; line base with baking parchment.
2 Combine dates, the water and soda in bowl of food processor; place lid on processor, let mixture stand 5 minutes.
3 Add sugar and butter to date mixture; process, by pulsing, about 5 seconds or until dates are roughly chopped.
4 Add eggs, then flour; process, by pulsing, about 10 seconds or until all ingredients are combined. Scrape any unmixed flour back into the mixture with a rubber spatula; pulse again to combine ingredients. Pour mixture into prepared tin.
5 Bake pudding about 55 minutes. Stand in tin 5 minutes before turning onto serving plate. Serve hot pudding with warm caramel sauce.

caramel sauce Combine sugar and butter in medium saucepan, stir over high heat; using wooden spoon, stir in cream. Once butter melts, bring sauce to a boil (to prevent it boiling over, either lower the heat or remove pan from heat for a moment). Stir sauce constantly until completely smooth; serve while warm.

serves 8

sticky date pudding with caramel sauce

apple crumble

5 large apples (1kg)
¼ cup (55g) caster sugar
¼ cup (60ml) water
crumble
½ cup (75g) self-raising flour
¼ cup (35g) plain flour
½ cup (110g) firmly packed brown
  sugar
100g cold butter, chopped
1 teaspoon ground cinnamon

1 Preheat oven to 180°C/160°C fan-assisted. Grease deep 1.5-litre baking dish.
2 Peel, core and quarter apples. Combine apple, sugar and the water in large saucepan; cook over low heat, covered, about 10 minutes. Drain; discard liquid.
3 Meanwhile, make crumble.
4 Place apples in dish; sprinkle with crumble. Bake about 25 minutes.
crumble Blend or process ingredients until combined.

serves 4

VARIATIONS
nut crumble Stir in ⅓ cup roasted slivered almonds and ⅓ cup coarsely chopped roasted hazelnuts to crumble mixture.
muesli crumble Prepare half the amount of basic crumble mixture; stir in 1 cup toasted muesli.

pear & rhubarb muesli crumble

4 medium pears (920g)
20g butter
¼ cup (50g) brown sugar
600g coarsely chopped rhubarb
2 tablespoons orange juice
1½ cups corn flakes, crushed
  slightly
½ cup (35g) rolled oats
½ cup (35g) shredded coconut
⅓ cup (75g) firmly packed brown
  sugar, extra
2 tablespoons plain flour
70g butter, coarsely chopped,
  extra

1 Preheat oven to 180°C/160°C fan-assisted.
2 Peel and core pears; cut into thick wedges. Melt butter in large saucepan; cook pear and sugar, stirring, until sugar dissolves and pear just starts to caramelise. Add rhubarb and juice; cook, stirring, until rhubarb is tender. Transfer mixture to 1.5-litre ovenproof dish.
3 Combine corn flakes, oats, coconut, extra sugar and flour in large bowl. Using fingers, rub extra butter into crumble mixture.

4 Spoon crumble mixture evenly over pear-rhubarb mixture; bake, uncovered, about 15 minutes or until crumble is golden brown. Serve with vanilla ice-cream, if desired.

serves 4

apple & marmalade streusel puddings

20g butter
4 medium apples (600g), peeled,
  cored, sliced thinly
2 tablespoons water
1 tablespoon caster sugar
½ cup (170g) orange marmalade
streusel topping
½ cup (75g) plain flour
¼ cup (35g) self-raising flour
⅓ cup (75g) firmly packed brown
  sugar
½ teaspoon ground cinnamon
100g butter, chopped

1 Make streusel topping.
2 Preheat oven to 200°C/180°C fan-assisted.
3 Melt butter in medium frying pan; cook apple, the water and sugar, stirring, about 10 minutes or until apple is tender. Stir in marmalade.
4 Grease four 180ml individual ovenproof dishes; divide apple mixture among dishes.

5 Coarsely grate streusel onto baking parchment; sprinkle over apple mixture. Bake about 20 minutes or until browned lightly.
streusel topping Blend or process all ingredients until combined. Roll into a ball; wrap in cling film. Freeze streusel about 1 hour or until firm.

serves 4

plum & pear amaretti crumble

825g can plums in syrup, drained,
  halved, stones removed
825g can pear halves in natural
  juice, drained, halved
1 teaspoon ground cardamom
125g amaretti, crushed
⅓ cup (50g) plain flour
⅓ cup (40g) ground almonds
½ cup (70g) slivered almonds
100g butter, chopped

1 Preheat oven to 200°C/180°C fan-assisted. Grease a deep 1.5-litre ovenproof dish.
2 Combine plums, pears and cardamom in dish; toss gently to combine.
3 Combine amaretti, flour, ground almonds and nuts in medium bowl. Using fingers, rub in butter; sprinkle evenly over plum mixture.
4 Bake, uncovered, about 15 minutes or until golden brown. Serve with cream or ice-cream, if desired.

serves 4

rice pudding

½ cup (100g) uncooked white
    medium-grain rice
2½ cups (625ml) milk
¼ cup (55g) caster sugar
¼ cup (40g) sultanas
½ teaspoon vanilla extract
2 teaspoons butter
½ teaspoon ground nutmeg

1 Preheat oven to 160°C/140°C
fan-assisted. Grease shallow 1-litre
baking dish.
2 Wash rice under cold water; drain
well. Combine rice, milk, sugar,
sultanas and extract in dish; whisk
lightly with fork. Dot with butter.
3 Bake, uncovered, 1 hour,
whisking lightly with fork under
skin occasionally. Sprinkle with
nutmeg; bake 20 minutes. Serve
warm or cold.

serves 6

creamed rice

1 litre (4 cups) milk
⅓ cup (75g) caster sugar
1 teaspoon vanilla extract
½ cup (100g) uncooked white
    medium-grain rice

1 Combine milk, sugar and extract
in large saucepan; bring to a boil.
Gradually add rice to boiling milk.
Reduce heat; simmer, covered,
stirring occasionally, about
50 minutes or until rice is tender
and milk is almost absorbed.
2 Serve warm or cold, with fresh
berries, if desired.

serves 4

baked apples

4 large Granny Smith apples (800g)
50g butter, melted
⅓ cup (75g) firmly packed brown
  sugar
½ cup (80g) sultanas
1 teaspoon ground cinnamon

1 Preheat oven to 160°C/140°C fan-assisted.
2 Core unpeeled apples about three-quarters of the way down from stem end, making hole 4cm in diameter. Use small sharp knife to score around centre of each apple.
3 Combine remaining ingredients in small bowl. Pack sultana mixture firmly into apples; stand apples upright in small baking dish. Bake, uncovered, about 45 minutes.

serves 4

VARIATIONS
muesli filling Replace sultana mixture with ⅔ cup muesli, 1 cup thawed, well-drained frozen blueberries, 40g melted butter and 2 tablespoons brown sugar.
berry filling Replace sultana mixture with 1½ cups thawed well-drained frozen mixed berries. Bruise 4 cardamom pods; place one cardamom pod in each apple with mixed berries.

sour cherry baked custards

1 cup (200g) drained canned
  morello cherries
3 eggs
1 teaspoon vanilla extract
½ cup (110g) caster sugar
2 cups (500ml) hot milk
2 teaspoons custard powder
1 tablespoon cold milk
½ teaspoon ground cinnamon

1 Preheat oven to 170°C/150°C fan-assisted.
2 Pat cherries dry with absorbent paper; divide among four shallow 180ml ovenproof dishes.
3 Whisk eggs, extract and sugar in medium bowl. Gradually whisk hot milk into egg mixture.
3 Blend custard powder with cold milk in small bowl until smooth; whisk into egg mixture.
5 Pour mixture over cherries; bake, uncovered, about 25 minutes or until just set. Serve warm or cooled sprinkled with cinnamon.

serves 4

baked custard

6 eggs
1 teaspoon vanilla extract
⅓ cup (75g) caster sugar
1 litre (4 cups) hot milk
¼ teaspoon ground nutmeg

1 Preheat oven to 160°C/140°C fan-assisted. Grease shallow 1.5-litre ovenproof dish.
2 Whisk eggs, extract and sugar in large bowl; gradually whisk in hot milk. Pour custard mixture into dish; sprinkle with nutmeg.
3 Place dish in larger baking dish; add enough boiling water to come halfway up sides of dish. Bake, uncovered, about 45 minutes. Remove custard from large dish; stand 5 minutes before serving.

serves 6

VARIATIONS

citrus Stir ½ teaspoon each of finely grated orange, lime and lemon rind into hot milk mixture; omit nutmeg.
chocolate Whisk 30g cocoa powder and 60g dark chocolate chips with eggs, extract and sugar; omit nutmeg.
coconut & cardamom Omit hot milk; bring 580ml milk, 400ml can coconut milk, 3 bruised cardamom pods and 5cm strip lime rind to a boil. Remove from heat, stand 10 minutes. Strain; discard solids. Whisk milk mixture into egg mixture.

baked rice custard

4 eggs
⅓ cup (75g) caster sugar
½ teaspoon vanilla extract
2 cups (500ml) milk
300ml double cream
⅓ cup (50g) raisins
1½ cups cold cooked white
    medium-grain rice
1 teaspoon ground cinnamon

1 Preheat oven to 180°C/160°C fan-assisted. Grease 1.5-litre baking dish.
2 Whisk eggs, sugar and extract in medium bowl until combined. Whisk in milk and cream; stir in raisins and rice.
3 Pour mixture into dish. Place dish in large baking dish; pour enough boiling water into baking dish to come halfway up sides of dish. Bake 30 minutes, whisking lightly with fork under skin occasionally. Sprinkle with cinnamon; bake 20 minutes. Serve warm or cold.

serves 6

crème caramel

¾ cup (165g) caster sugar
½ cup (125ml) water
300ml double cream
1¾ cups (430ml) milk
6 eggs
1 teaspoon vanilla extract
⅓ cup (75g) caster sugar, extra

1 Preheat oven to 160°C/140°C fan-assisted.
2 Combine sugar and the water in medium frying pan; stir over heat, without boiling, until sugar dissolves. Bring to a boil; boil, uncovered, without stirring, until mixture is deep caramel in colour. Remove from heat; allow bubbles to subside. Pour toffee into deep 20cm-round cake tin.
3 Combine cream and milk in medium saucepan; bring to a boil. Whisk eggs, extract and extra sugar in large bowl; whisking constantly, pour hot milk mixture into egg mixture. Strain mixture into cake tin.
4 Place tin in medium baking dish; add enough boiling water to come half way up side of tin. Bake, uncovered, about 40 minutes or until firm. Remove custard from baking dish, cover; refrigerate overnight.
5 Gently ease crème caramel from side of tin; invert onto deep-sided serving plate.

serves 6

VARIATIONS
vanilla pod Add 1 split vanilla pod to cream and milk mixture before bringing to a boil; strain, remove vanilla pod before adding to egg mixture.
cinnamon Add 1 cinnamon stick to cream and milk mixture before bringing to a boil; strain, remove cinnamon stick before adding to egg mixture.
orange Stir 2 teaspoons finely grated orange rind into custard mixture before baking.
hazelnut Add 1 cup (120g) coarsely chopped roasted hazelnuts to cream and milk mixture; bring to a boil. Cover; stand 20 minutes then strain through muslin-lined sieve. Discard nuts. Bring cream and milk mixture back to a boil before whisking into egg mixture.

crème brûlée

1 vanilla pod
3 cups (750ml) whipping cream
6 egg yolks
¼ cup (55g) caster sugar
¼ cup (40g) icing sugar

1 Preheat oven to 180°C/160°C fan-assisted. Grease six 125ml individual ovenproof dishes.
2 Split vanilla pod in half lengthways; scrape seeds into medium heatproof bowl. Heat pod with cream in small saucepan, without boiling.
3 Add egg yolks and caster sugar to seeds in bowl; gradually whisk in hot cream mixture. Set bowl over medium saucepan of simmering water; stir over heat about 10 minutes or until custard mixture thickens slightly and coats the back of a spoon; discard pod.
4 Place dishes in large baking dish; divide custard among dishes. Add enough boiling water to baking dish to come halfway up sides of ovenproof dishes. Bake, uncovered, about 20 minutes or until custard sets. Remove custards from dish; cool. Cover; refrigerate overnight.

5 Preheat grill. Place custards in shallow flameproof dish filled with ice cubes; sprinkle custards evenly with sifted icing sugar. Using finger, spread sugar over the surface of each custard, pressing in gently; grill until tops of crème brûlée caramelise.

serves 6

VARIATION
sugar crusted crème brûlée
Replace icing sugar with ¼ cup caster sugar, 2 tablespoons brown sugar and 2 tablespoons grated palm sugar.

apricot & honey soufflés

¼ cup (55g) caster sugar
4 apricots (200g)
¼ cup (60ml) water
2 tablespoons honey
4 egg whites

1 Preheat oven to 180°C/160°C fan-assisted. Grease six 180ml individual soufflé dishes; sprinkle inside of dishes with a little of the sugar, place on oven tray.
2 Place apricots in small heatproof bowl, cover with boiling water; stand 2 minutes. Drain; cool 5 minutes. Peel and deseed apricots; chop flesh finely.

3 Combine apricots in small saucepan with remaining sugar, the water and honey; bring to a boil. Reduce heat; simmer, uncovered, about 10 minutes or until apricots soften to a jam-like consistency.
4 Beat egg whites in small bowl with electric mixer until soft peaks form. With motor operating, gradually add hot apricot mixture, beating until just combined.
5 Divide soufflé mixture among dishes; bake 15 minutes. Dust with icing sugar, if desired.

serves 6

chocolate soufflés

⅓ cup (75g) caster sugar
50g butter
1 tablespoon plain flour
200g dark eating chocolate, melted
2 egg yolks
4 egg whites

1 Preheat oven to 180°C/160°C fan-assisted. Grease four 180ml individual soufflé dishes. Sprinkle inside of dishes with a little of the sugar; shake away excess. Place dishes on oven tray.

2 Melt butter in small saucepan, add flour; cook, stirring, about 2 minutes or until mixture thickens and bubbles. Remove from heat; stir in chocolate and egg yolks. Transfer to large bowl.
3 Beat egg whites in small bowl with electric mixer until soft peaks form. Gradually add remaining sugar, beating until sugar dissolves. Fold egg white mixture into chocolate mixture, in two batches.
4 Divide soufflé mixture among dishes; bake 15 minutes. Dust with cocoa powder, if desired.

serves 4

strawberry marshmallow pavlova

4 egg whites
1 cup (220g) caster sugar
½ teaspoon vanilla extract
¾ teaspoon white vinegar
300ml whipping cream, whipped
250g strawberries, halved

1 Preheat oven to 120°C/100°C fan-assisted. Line oven tray with foil; grease foil, dust with cornflour, shake away excess. Mark 18cm-circle on foil.
2 Beat egg whites in small bowl with electric mixer until soft peaks form; gradually add sugar, beating until sugar dissolves. Add extract and vinegar; beat until combined.
3 Spread meringue into circle on foil, building up at the side to 8cm in height.

4 Smooth side and top of pavlova gently. Using spatula blade, mark decorative grooves around side of pavlova; smooth top again.
5 Bake about 1½ hours. Turn off oven; cool pavlova in oven with door ajar. When pavlova is cold, cut around top edge (the crisp meringue top will fall slightly on top of the marshmallow). Serve pavlova topped with whipped cream and strawberries; dust lightly with sifted icing sugar, if desired.

serves 8

chocolate berry meringues

3 egg whites
¾ cup (165g) caster sugar
1 tablespoon cocoa powder
300ml whipping cream
150g fresh raspberries
250g fresh strawberries, quartered
150g fresh blueberries

1 Preheat oven to 120°C/100°C fan-assisted. Grease and line oven tray with baking parchment. Draw four 13cm-diameter circles on paper.

2 Beat egg whites in small bowl with electric mixer until soft peaks form. Add sugar, 1 tablespoon at a time, beating until sugar dissolves between each addition; fold in sifted cocoa.
3 Spread meringue mixture over drawn circles. Bake about 45 minutes or until firm; cool meringues in oven with door ajar.
4 Beat cream in small bowl with electric mixer until lightly whipped; top meringues with cream and berries.

serves 4

4 egg whites
1 cup (220g) caster sugar
1 teaspoon orange flower water
300ml whipping cream
pomegranate syrup
2 tablespoons caster sugar
2 tablespoons water
½ cup (125ml) pomegranate pulp

1 Preheat oven to 120°C/100°C fan-assisted. Grease six-hole (180ml) large muffin pan; line each pan hole with two criss-crossed 5cm x 20cm strips of baking parchment.
2 Beat egg whites in small bowl with electric mixer until soft peaks form; gradually add sugar, beating until sugar dissolves. Beat in orange flower water until combined.
3 Divide meringue among pan holes; use the back of a spoon to create a swirl on top. Bake about 30 minutes. Turn off oven; cool meringues in oven with door ajar.
4 Meanwhile, make pomegranate syrup.
5 Using baking parchment strips, remove meringues from pan. Serve, top-side up, with pomegranate syrup and whipped cream.

pomegranate syrup Stir sugar and the water in small saucepan over heat until sugar dissolves; bring to the boil. Boil, uncovered, about 2 minutes or until thickened slightly. Add pulp; simmer 2 minutes. Cool.

makes 6
tip You need two medium pomegranates (640g) to get the required amount of pomegranate pulp for this recipe.

orange blossom meringues with pomegranate syrup

warm chocolate pavlovas

2 egg whites
1⅓ cups (215g) icing sugar
⅓ cup (80ml) boiling water
1 tablespoon cocoa powder, sifted
500ml chocolate ice-cream
chocolate custard sauce
1 tablespoon cornflour
1 tablespoon cocoa powder, sifted
1 tablespoon caster sugar
1 cup (125ml) milk
2 egg yolks

1 Preheat oven to 180°C/160°C fan-assisted. Line large oven tray with baking parchment.
2 Beat egg whites, icing sugar and the water in small bowl with electric mixer about 10 minutes or until firm peaks form.
3 Fold sifted cocoa into meringue. Drop six equal amounts of mixture onto tray; use the back of a spoon to create well in centre of mounds. Bake about 25 minutes or until firm to touch.
4 Meanwhile, make chocolate custard sauce.
5 Serve pavlovas straight from the oven, topped with ice-cream and sauce.

chocolate custard sauce Blend cornflour, cocoa and sugar with milk in small saucepan. Stir in egg yolks. Stir over heat until sauce boils and thickens.

serves 4

4 egg whites
1 cup (220g) caster sugar
1 tablespoon cornflour
⅔ cup (160ml) thick cream
vanilla strawberries
1 cup (220g) caster sugar
½ cup (125ml) water
2 teaspoons vanilla extract
500g strawberries, halved

1 Preheat oven to 120°C/100°C fan-assisted. Grease two oven trays; line with baking parchment. Draw eight 8cm rounds on baking parchment.
2 Beat egg whites in small bowl with electric mixer until soft peaks form. Gradually add sugar; beat until sugar dissolves between additions. Beat in sifted cornflour.
3 Spoon meringue mixture into rounds; make hollows in meringue using back of a dessertspoon. Bake pavlovas about 1¼ hours. Cool pavlovas in oven with door ajar.
4 Make vanilla strawberries.
5 Serve pavlovas topped with cream and strawberries.
vanilla strawberries Combine sugar and the water in small saucepan. Stir over heat until sugar dissolves; bring to the boil. Boil, uncovered, without stirring, 2 minutes. Remove from heat; stir in extract. Place strawberries in medium bowl; stir in syrup. Cool.

makes 8
tip The cream used here is thick pure cream (containing 66 percent fat), which doesn't need to be whipped. Just spoon it out of its container onto the pavlovas.

mini pavlovas with vanilla strawberries

berry cream roulade

3 eggs
½ cup (110g) caster sugar
½ cup (75g) cornflour
1 tablespoon custard powder
1 teaspoon cream of tartar
½ teaspoon bicarbonate of soda
1 tablespoon caster sugar, extra
1 tablespoon icing sugar
berry cream
¾ cup (180ml) whipping cream
1 teaspoon vanilla extract
1 tablespoon icing sugar
1 cup (150g) frozen blackberries,
  chopped coarsely

1 Preheat oven to 180°C/160°C fan-assisted. Grease 25cm x 30cm swiss roll tin; line base and two long sides with baking parchment, extending paper 5cm over long sides.
2 Beat eggs and caster sugar in small bowl with electric mixer about 5 minutes or until sugar is dissolved and mixture is thick and creamy; transfer to large bowl.
3 Sift cornflour, custard powder, cream of tartar and soda together twice onto paper then sift over egg mixture; gently fold dry ingredients into egg mixture. Spread sponge mixture into tin; bake about 12 minutes.
4 Meanwhile, place a piece of baking parchment cut the same size as swiss roll tin on bench; sprinkle evenly with extra caster sugar.
5 Turn sponge onto sugared paper; peel away lining paper. Use serrated knife to cut away crisp edges from all sides of sponge, cover sponge with a tea towel; cool.
6 Meanwhile, make berry cream; spread cream over sponge. Using paper as a guide, roll sponge gently from long side to enclose filling. Dust with sifted icing sugar.

berry cream Beat cream, extract and icing sugar in small bowl with electric mixer until soft peaks form; fold in thawed berries.

VARIATION
This sponge can also be made in a 22cm-round cake tin, greased with butter and floured lightly, and baked in a 180°C/160°C fan-assisted oven about 20 minutes. Turn sponge, top-side up, onto a baking-parchment-covered wire rack. Split the sponge in half and join the halves with berry cream.

tiramisu roulade

2 tablespoons coffee-flavoured
  liqueur
¼ cup (60ml) water
2 tablespoons caster sugar
1 tablespoon instant coffee
  granules
1 tablespoon boiling water
3 eggs
½ cup (110g) caster sugar, extra
½ cup (75g) plain flour
2 tablespoons flaked almonds
coffee liqueur cream
1 cup (250g) mascarpone
½ cup (125ml) whipping cream
2 tablespoons coffee-flavoured
  liqueur

1 Preheat oven to 220°C/200°C fan-assisted. Grease 25cm x 30cm swiss roll tin; line base and two long sides with baking parchment, extending paper 5cm over long sides.
2 Combine liqueur with the water and sugar in small saucepan; bring to a boil. Reduce heat; simmer, uncovered, without stirring, about 5 minutes or until syrup thickens slightly. Remove from heat, stir in half of the coffee; reserve syrup.
3 Dissolve remaining coffee in the boiling water.
4 Beat eggs and extra sugar in small bowl with electric mixer about 5 minutes or until sugar is dissolved and mixture is thick; transfer to large bowl, fold in dissolved coffee.
5 Meanwhile, sift flour twice onto paper. Sift flour over egg mixture then fold gently into mixture. Spread sponge mixture into tin; sprinkle with almonds. Bake about 15 minutes.
6 Meanwhile, place a piece of baking parchment cut the same size as swiss roll tin on bench; sprinkle evenly with about 2 teaspoons of caster sugar. Turn sponge onto sugared paper; peel away lining paper. Use serrated knife to cut crisp edges from all sides of sponge. Roll sponge from long side, using paper as guide; cool.

7 Meanwhile, beat ingredients for coffee liqueur cream in small bowl with electric mixer until firm peaks form. Unroll sponge, brush with reserved syrup. Spread cream over sponge then re-roll sponge. Cover roulade with cling film; refrigerate 30 minutes before serving.

serves 8
tip Use whatever coffee-flavoured liqueur you prefer in the mascarpone cream filling, or consider using chocolate, almond or hazelnut, liquorice or even mint-flavoured liqueur.

tips & techniques

MEASURING

All our measures are level. To use a measuring cup properly for dry ingredients, shake the ingredient loosely into the cup, don't pack it in, unless the recipe directs you to do this. Level off the surface carefully with the blade of a knife or metal spatula.

GREASING & FLOURING TINS

Cake tins need greasing, even non-stick surfaces need a light greasing. You can use cooking oil spray, or melted butter or margarine. Use a pastry brush to grease the tins evenly. Sprinkle a little flour into the tin; shake, tap and then turn the tin until the surface is evenly floured. Tap the tin, upside-down, to get rid of the excess flour.

TESTING CAKES

You can use a skewer to test most cakes (not sponges or fruit cakes). Remove the cake from the oven, close the oven door, push a skewer gently through the thickest part of the cake to the bottom of the tin. Pull the skewer out: if the skewer is clean the cake is done; if the skewer has uncooked mixture on it, cook the cake further.

cakes

LINING CAKE TINS

Grease the cake tin evenly, with either cooking-oil spray or melted butter or margarine. The greasing will ensure that the cake turns out of the pan nicely, also, it will hold the lining paper in place.

TRACING AND CUTTING THE LINING PAPER

Using the base of the tin as a guide, trace around the tin onto the lining paper. Cut out the shape, slightly inside the tracing. Cut a strip of paper long enough to cover the side of the tin in one piece, and overlap a little at the ends. The strip needs to be wide enough to cover the sides, plus about 2cm for the base, plus about 5cm to extend the paper above the sides of the tin.

LINING THE TIN

Make a fold about 2cm wide, along one of the long sides of the strip of paper. Snip along the strip, up to the fold, at about 2cm intervals. Position the long strip of paper around the inside of the tin, then position the base-lining paper in the bottom of the tin.

cakes

COOLING CAKES
Most cakes are turned out of their tins (after a few minutes of standing) onto wire racks to cool. Sponges are always turned out of their tins as soon as they come out of the oven onto a baking-parchment-covered wire rack. Rich fruit cakes are usually cooled in their tins.

INVERTING CAKES
To invert a ckes safely, place another wire rack on top of the cake, sandwiching the cake between the two racks, then carefully turn the cake right way up.

SYRUPING CAKES
Syrup cakes almost always have hot syrup poured over them when they're hot. Sometimes the syrup is poured over them while they're still in their cake tins, sometimes the cakes are turned out. In this case, the wire rack has a tray placed under it to catch the drips of syrup. This overflow syrup should be poured back over the cake.

muffins

MUFFIN PANS

There are several different-sized muffin pans available, from supermarkets or kitchenware shops. The most common pans available are mini, large (or texas) and standard-sized. Muffin pans need to be greased or lined with paper cases to fit the various sized pans. Either coat the pan holes evenly with cooking oil spray, or brush the pan holes evenly with a little melted butter.

SPOONING THE MIXTURE

Using a two spoons, or a spoon and one of your fingers, divide the mixture evenly into the holes of the pan. The recipes will tell you how much to put into the pans, but, as a guide, they usually need to be about two-thirds full.

BAKING MUFFINS

Be guided by individual recipes, but generally, standard-sized muffins are baked in a moderately hot oven (200°C/180°C fan-assisted) for about 20 minutes, the large-sized muffins take longer, and the mini-sized muffins less time to bake. They are done when they shrink slightly from the side of the pan holes. Turn them onto a wire rack to cool.

biscuits

BISCUITS

Always allow some space for biscuits to spread during cooking. The amount of spreading depends on the raising agent in the recipe and the consistency of the mixture. Bake biscuits either on a greased tray or baking-parchment-lined tray. We grease under the baking parchment to hold the parchment in position, but this isn't really necessary.

FLATTENING BISCUITS

A lot of recipes call for biscuits to be flattened slightly in some way. This can be done by hand, or, like the picture, done with the floured tines of a fork.

TO TEST IF BISCUITS ARE COOKED

Inexperienced bakers tend to overcook biscuits. The best and easiest way to make sure they're done is to check the cooking time, then, look at them to see if they're browned and firm, then, give one biscuit a gentle push on the tray with your thumb or finger. If the biscuit moves, even if it's still soft, they're done, they'll firm as they cool.

palmiers

MAKING PALMIERS
These are so easy to make, with store-bought frozen puff pastry, which takes only a little time to thaw, ready to roll and shape. Follow recipes for any flavourings, fillings, etc., or invent some of your own. Roll one side of the pastry towards the middle of the sheet, then roll the other side to meet in the middle.

FOLDING PALMIERS
Press the two rolled up sides together so they join in the middle.

CUTTING PALMIERS
Using a sharp knife, cut the palmier shapes crossways into about 1cm pieces, place them on baking-parchment-lined oven trays, allowing room for them to spread. Bake as directed in the recipe.

eggs

BEATING EGG WHITES

To beat egg whites with an electric mixer, the beaters and bowl must be clean and dry; whites will not beat up if they're in touch with fat. Use a deep, not wide, bowl so the beaters can get into the whites to create volume. Start beating on a low speed, gradually increasing the speed as the whites thicken to the correct stage for the recipe.

FOLDING-IN EGG WHITES

This is a skill you must learn if you're going to become a good baker. It can be tricky when folding whites into a heavy mixture (such as chocolate or cake batter), or a lot of mixture. To loosen such mixtures, fold about a quarter of the whites through, using a spatula or whisk, then fold half the remaining whites through. The action of folding means that you have to pull the ingredients together in such a way that you keep the air in the mixture. We prefer to use a rubber spatula for this, as you can scrape the side of the bowl, as you fold the ingredients together.

FRIANDS

Egg whites used for friands must not be beaten too much at all, use a whisk, or a fork, it doesn't really matter. The important thing is not to beat air into the whites, they simply need to be broken up evenly. Air only creates pockets, bubbles and tunnels in the dense friand mixture.

chocolate

MELTING CHOCOLATE

Chocolate must be melted carefully and gently. The following method is the safest: place a heatproof bowl (preferably glass or china) containing the roughly chopped chocolate over a pan of barely simmering water. The water must never touch the base of the bowl or the chocolate will 'seize'. Stir chocolate occasionally until smooth, remove from the pan as soon as it has melted.

GANACHE

Ganache, a decadent mixture of milk, dark or white chocolate and cream, is mostly used for frosting or filling, It can be used as a coating –in this case, the mixture is cooled but used before it thickens. When it's used as a frosting or filling the ganache is cooled, sometimes in the fridge, it needs an occasional stir with a wooden spoon to mix the ingredients. It can also be whipped after it has been refrigerated.

Making chocolate curls

The simplest and easiest way to make chocolate curls is with a vegetable peeler. You will only be able to make small curls, but they're quick and easy, and you can curl the chocolate straight onto the surface of the cake. Use a large bar or piece of chocolate, at room temperature, and drag the peeler along the side of the bar. To make larger curls, spread melted chocolate evenly and thinly onto a piece of marble, laminated board or flat oven tray; stand at room temperature until just set but not hard. Pull a melon baller over the surface of chocolate to make curls.

pastry

ROLLING OUT PASTRY

Dust the work surface lightly but evenly with flour, or you can sometimes use sugar for sweet dough; this prevents pastry from sticking. Keep some flour in a dredger (mug with pierced lid) for this purpose. Dust rolling pin with flour, or roll dough between sheets of greaseproof or baking parchment. Roll from centre out, lifting and turning dough a quarter-turn. Never turn dough over.

LINING A TIN WITH PASTRY

Dust pastry lightly with flour, roll loosely around lightly floured rolling pin and unroll over pan. Ease in gently, taking care not to stretch it; press to fit. Prick holes in the uncooked dough so that it will not puff up when baked. You can use a docker – a spiked roller – to do this, or you can use a fork to prick the pastry all over. Trim edges and rest pastry in the refrigerator before baking.

BAKING BLIND

A pastry case can be baked blind (empty) to ensure the pastry will not become soggy from the filling and will remain crisp. Line with baking parchment and weigh down with raw rice or dried beans, then bake as directed. The rice and beans can be reused for blind baking but not eating.

pastry

FLUTING
To flute the edge of a tart shell or pie crust, press from just inside the edge with a thumb pinched between the other thumb and finger. For a sunburst effect, press edge flat and cut 1cm slits around crust at 2cm intervals.

TRIMMING PUFF PASTRY
Hold the pie plate up in one hand, and, using a large sharp knife, cut any overhanging pastry away from the plate edge, at a 45° angle. To help the puff pastry flake, use the blade of a sharp knife to 'cut' the side surface of the joined pastry edge. This will encourage the pastry to flake, after the slightly squashing effect of trimming the edge.

STORING AND FREEZING
Pastry can be stored, tightly wrapped in cling film and enclosed in a plastic bag, in the refrigerator for up to a week, or frozen for up to a month. Allow the pastry to return to room temperature before rolling or shaping.

glossary

allspice also known as pimento or Jamaican pepper; available whole or ground.
almonds
blanched skins removed.
caramelised (Vienna almonds), toffee-coated almonds.
essence often interchangeable with **extract**; made with almond oil and alcohol or another agent.
flaked paper-thin slices.
ground also known as almond meal; nuts are powdered to a coarse flour texture.
slivered cut lengthways.
amaretti small Italian-style macaroons (biscuit or cookie) made with ground almonds.
aniseed also called anise; the liquorice-flavoured seeds of the anise plant.

bicarbonate of soda also called baking soda.
blood orange a virtually seedless citrus fruit with blood-red-streaked rind and flesh; sweet, non-acidic, salmon-coloured pulp and juice wtih slight strawberry or raspberry overtones. The rind is not as bitter as an ordinary orange.
bran, unprocessed is the coarse outer husk of cereal grains, and can be found in health food stores and supermarkets.
brazil nuts native to South America, a triangular-shelled oily nut with an unusually tender white flesh and a mild, rich flavour. Good for eating as well as cooking, the nuts can be eaten raw or cooked, or can be ground into meal for baking.

brioche rich French yeast-risen bread made with butter and eggs.
buttermilk fresh low-fat milk cultured to give a slightly sour, tangy taste; low-fat yogurt or milk can be substituted.

cardamom can be bought in pod, seed or ground form. Has a distinctive, aromatic, sweetly rich flavour.
cherries, morello the sour variety used in jams, preserves, pies and savoury dishes, particularly as an accompaniment to game birds.
chocolate
chips hold their shape in baking.
dark eating made of cocoa liquor, cocoa butter and sugar.
hazelnut spread we use Nutella. It was originally developed when chocolate was hard to source during World War II; hazelnuts were added to extend the chocolate supply.
milk eating most popular eating chocolate, mild and very sweet; similar in make-up to dark, but with the addition of milk solids.
white eating contains no cocoa solids, deriving its sweet flavour from cocoa butter. Is very sensitive to heat.
ciabatta meaning 'slipper' in Italian, the traditional shape of this popular crisp-crusted white bread.
cinnamon dried inner bark of the shoots of the cinnamon tree. Available as a stick or ground.
cloves can be used whole or in ground form. Has a strong scent and taste so should be used minimally.

cocoa powder also known as unsweetened cocoa; cocoa beans that have been fermented, roasted, shelled, ground into powder then cleared of most of the fat content.
coconut
cream available in tins and cartons; as a rule, the proportions are two parts coconut to one part water.
desiccated unsweetened and concentrated, dried finely shredded.
flaked dried flaked coconut flesh.
shredded thin strips of dried coconut.
coffee-flavoured liqueur we use either Kahlua or Tia Maria coffee-flavoured liqueur.
corn syrup a sweet syrup made by heating cornstarch with water under pressure. It comes in light and dark types and is used in baking and in confectionery. It is sometimes mixed with other sugars such as honey.
cornflour also known as cornstarch; used as a thickening agent in cooking.
cream cheese a soft cow's-milk cheese with a fat content ranging from 14 per cent to 33 per cent.
cream we used fresh cream in this book, unless otherwise stated. Also known as pure cream and pouring cream; has no additives unlike commercially thickened cream. Minimum fat content 35%.
soured a thick commercially-cultured soured cream. Minimum fat content 35%.
whipping a cream that contains a thickener. Has a minimum fat content of 35 per cent.

cream of tartar the acid ingredient in baking powder; added to confectionery mixtures to help prevent sugar from crystallising. Keeps frostings creamy and improves volume when beating egg whites.

date fruit of the date palm tree, eaten fresh or dried, on their own or in prepared dishes. About 4cm to 6cm in length, oval and plump, thin-skinned, with a honey-sweet flavour and sticky texture.

dulce de leche a caramel sauce made from milk and sugar. Can be used straight from the jar for cheesecakes, slices and tarts. Has similar qualities to sweetened condensed milk, only a thicker, caramel consistency; great to use in caramel desserts.

essences are synthetically produced substances used in small amounts to impart their respective flavours to foods. Extracts are made by actually extracting the flavour from a food product. In the case of vanilla, pods are soaked, usually in alcohol, to capture the authentic flavour. Both extracts and essences will keep indefinitely if stored in a cool dark place.

figs small, soft, pear-shaped fruit with a sweet pulpy flesh full of tiny edible seeds. Vary in skin and flesh colour according to type, not ripeness; when ripe, figs should be unblemished and bursting with flavour; nectar beads at the base indicate when a fig is at its best. Figs may also be glacéd (candied), dried or canned in sugar syrup.

filo pastry chilled or frozen tissue-thin pastry sheets that are very versatile, lending themselves to both sweet and savoury dishes.

flour

plain all-purpose flour.

rice extremely fine flour made from ground rice.

self-raising plain flour sifted with baking powder (a raising agent consisting mainly of 2 parts cream of tartar to 1 part bicarbonate of soda) in the proportion of 150g flour to 2 level teaspoons baking powder.

wholemeal also known as wholewheat flour; milled with the wheat germ so is higher in fibre and more nutritional than plain flour.

food colouring vegetable-based substance available in liquid, paste or gel form.

gelatine we used powdered gelatine; also available in sheet form known as leaf gelatine.

ginger

fresh also called green or root ginger; the thick gnarled root of a tropical plant. Can be kept, peeled, covered with dry sherry in a jar and refrigerated, or frozen in an airtight container.

stem fresh ginger root preserved in sugar syrup.

ground also known as powdered ginger; used as a flavouring in cakes, pies and puddings, but cannot be substituted for fresh ginger.

glacé cherries also known as candied cherries; boiled in heavy sugar syrup and then dried. Used in cakes, breads and sweets.

glacé fruit fruit such as peaches, pineapple, orange and citron cooked in heavy sugar syrup then dried.

golden syrup a by-product of refined sugarcane; pure maple syrup or honey can be substituted.

hazelnuts also known as filberts; plump, grape-sized, rich, sweet nut having a brown skin that is removed by rubbing heated nuts together vigorously in a tea-towel.

ground made by grinding hazelnuts to a coarse flour texture for use in baking or as a thickening agent.

hazelnut-flavoured liqueur we used frangelico.

macadamias native to Australia, a rich and buttery nut; store in refrigerator because of its high oil content.

maple syrup distilled from the sap of maple trees found only in Canada and parts of North America. Maple-flavoured syrup is not an adequate substitute for the real thing.

mascarpone a cultured cream product made in much the same way as yogurt. It's whitish to creamy yellow in colour, with a soft, creamy texture.

milk

condensed a canned milk product consisting of milk with more than half the water content removed and sugar added to the milk that remains.

evaporated, low-fat we used canned milk with 1.6g fat per 100ml.

mixed peel candied citrus peel.

mixed spice a blend of ground spices usually consisting of cinnamon, allspice and nutmeg.

muesli also known as granola; a combination of grains (mainly oats), nuts and dried fruits.

nutmeg dried nut of an evergreen tree; available in ground form or you can grate your own with a fine grater.

oat bran the hard and rather woody protective coating of oats which serves to protect the grain before it germinates.

oil, vegetable Any number of oils sourced from plants rather than animal fats.

orange-flavoured liqueur you can use any orange-flavoured liqueur: Grand Marnier, Cointreau, Curaçao are all suitable.

orange flower water concentrated flavouring made from orange blossoms.

passionfruit also known as granadilla; a small tropical fruit, native to Brazil, comprised of a tough dark-purple skin surrounding edible black sweet-sour seeds.

pecans Native to the United States; golden-brown, buttery and rich.

Good in savoury and sweet dishes; especially good in salads.

pine nuts also known as pignoli; small, cream-coloured kernels obtained from the cones of different varieties of pine trees.

pistachios pale green, delicately flavoured nut inside hard off-white shells. To peel, soak shelled nuts in boiling water about 5 minutes; drain, then pat dry.

polenta a flour-like cereal made of ground corn (maize); similar to cornmeal but finer and lighter in colour; also the name of the dish made from it.

pomegranate dark-red, leathery-skinned fresh fruit about the size of an orange filled with hundreds of seeds, each wrapped in an edible lucent-crimson pulp having a unique tangy sweet-sour flavour.

poppy seeds small, dried, bluish-grey seeds of the poppy plant. Poppy seeds have a crunchy texture and a nutty flavour. Available whole or ground in most supermarkets.

prunes commercially or sun-dried plums; store in the fridge.

raisins dried sweet grapes (traditionally muscatel grapes).

rolled oats traditional whole oat grains that have been steamed and flattened. Not the quick-cook variety.

rosewater extract made from crushed rose petals; available from health food stores and speciality grocers.

semolina a hard part of the wheat which is sifted out and used mainly for making pasta.

star anise a dried star-shaped pod, the seeds of which taste of aniseed.

sugar we used coarse, granulated table sugar, also known as crystal sugar, unless otherwise specified.

brown an extremely soft, fine granulated sugar retaining molasses for its deep colour and flavour.

caster also known as superfine or finely granulated table sugar.

demerara small-grained golden-coloured crystal sugar.

icing also known as confectioners' sugar or powdered sugar.

raw natural brown granulated sugar.

sultanas also known as golden raisins; dried seedless white grapes.

treacle thick, dark syrup not unlike molasses; a by-product of sugar refining.

vanilla

essence obtained from vanilla beans infused in alcohol and water.

extract obtained from vanilla beans infused in water; a non-alcoholic version of essence.

pod dried long, thin pod from a tropical golden orchid grown in central and South America and Tahiti; the minuscule black seeds inside the bean are used to impart a distinctively sweet vanilla flavour.

vinegar

malt made from fermented malt and beech shavings.

white made from spirit of cane sugar.

yogurt an unflavoured, full-fat cow's milk yogurt has been used in these recipes unless stated otherwise.

index

conversion chart

measures

One Australian metric measuring cup holds approximately 250ml; one Australian metric tablespoon holds 20ml; one Australian metric teaspoon holds 5ml.

All cup and spoon measurements are level. The most accurate way of measuring dry ingredients is to weigh them. When measuring liquids, use a clear glass or plastic jug with the metric markings.

We use large eggs with an average weight of 60g. This book contains recipes for dishes made with raw or lightly cooked eggs. These should be avoided by vulnerable people such as pregnant and nursing mothers, invalids, the elderly, babies and young children.

dry measures

METRIC	IMPERIAL
15g	½oz
30g	1oz
60g	2oz
90g	3oz
125g	4oz (¼lb)
155g	5oz
185g	6oz
220g	7oz
250g	8oz (½lb)
280g	9oz
315g	10oz
345g	11oz
375g	12oz (¾lb)
410g	13oz
440g	14oz
470g	15oz
500g	16oz (1lb)
750g	24oz (1½lb)
1kg	32oz (2lb)

liquid measures

METRIC	IMPERIAL
30ml	1 fluid oz
60ml	2 fluid oz
100ml	3 fluid oz
125ml	4 fluid oz
150ml	5 fluid oz (¼ pint/1 gill)
190ml	6 fluid oz
250ml	8 fluid oz
300ml	10 fluid oz (½ pint)
500ml	16 fluid oz
600ml	20 fluid oz (1 pint)
1000ml (1 litre)	1¾ pints

length measures

METRIC	IMPERIAL
3mm	⅛in
6mm	¼in
1cm	½in
2cm	¾in
2.5cm	1in
5cm	2in
6cm	2½in
8cm	3in
10cm	4in
13cm	5in
15cm	6in
18cm	7in
20cm	8in
23cm	9in
25cm	10in
28cm	11in
30cm	12in (1ft)

oven temperatures

These oven temperatures are only a guide for conventional ovens. For fan-forced ovens, check the manufacturer's manual.

	°C (CELSIUS)	°F (FAHRENHEIT)	GAS MARK
Very low	120	250	½
Low	150	275-300	1-2
Moderately low	160	325	3
Moderate	180	350-375	4-5
Moderately hot	200	400	6
Hot	220	425-450	7-8
Very hot	240	475	9

4